The Closed Faith

The Grand Tour

The Closed Faith

Flavio Conti

Translated by Patrick Creagh

HBJ Press
a subsidiary of Harcourt Brace Jovanovich, Inc.
New York

HBJ Press

President, Robert J. George

Publisher, Giles Kemp

Vice President, Richard S. Perkins, Jr.

Managing Director, Valerie S. Hopkins

Executive Editor, Marcia Heath

Series Editor, Carolyn Hall

Staff Editor, Chris Heath

Text Editors: Jack Beatty, Carole Cook, Ernest
  Kohlmetz, Nancy Nies, Joyce Milton

Editorial Production: Karen E. English, Ann
  McGrath, Eric Brus, Betsie Brownell,
  Patricia Leal, Pamela George

Project Coordinator, Linda S. Behrens

Business Manager, Richard White

Marketing Director, John R. Whitman

Public Relations, Janet Schotta

Business Staff: Pamela Herlich, Joan Kenney

Architectural Consultant, Dennis J. DeWitt

Text Consultants: Janet Adams, Perween
  Hasan, James Weirick

Design Implementation, Designworks

Rizzoli Editore

Authors of the Italian Edition: Anco Ancev,
  Dr. Flavio Conti, Paolo Favole, G. M.
  Tabarelli, Bruna Vielmi

Idea and Realization, Harry C. Lindinger

General Supervisor, Luigi U. Re

Graphic Designer, Gerry Valsecchi

Photography Credits:
Cauchetier: pp. 9–32 / *Hassmann:* p. 105, pp. 108–116 / *Jus
Autor:* pp. 153–155, p. 156 top, center, and bottom left, p.
158 / *Klammet & Aberl:* pp. 106–107 / *Magnum-Morath:* p.
66 bottom / *Magnum-Rodger:* pp. 58–59 / *Martin:* p. 137,
p. 140 top, left, and right, p. 141, p. 142 bottom left and
right, p. 143 top, p. 146, p. 148 / *O.P.I.–Orlandi:* p. 77 bottom, p. 83 left / *Oronoz:* p. 140 bottom, p. 144 top left and
bottom right, p. 145 / *Pubbliaerfoto:* pp. 74–75, pp. 42–
43 / *Ricciarini–Simion:* p. 156 bottom right, p. 157, pp.
159–164 / *Rizzoli:* pp. 122–123, p. 124 top, center, and bottom right / p. 126 bottom, pp. 127–128, pp. 130–132, pp.
84–85, pp. 90–91 / *Salmer:* pp. 138–139, p. 142 top left, p.
143 bottom, p. 144 bottom left, p. 147 / *Scala:* p. 121, p. 124
bottom left, p. 125, p. 126 top, p. 129, p. 73, p. 76, pp. 80–82,
p. 83 bottom right, p. 87 right, p. 88, p. 89 bottom left and
right, pp. 92–96 / *Scala-Scarfiotti:* p. 65 top right / *T.
Schneiders:* p. 79 top / *S.E.F.:* p. 78, p. 86, p. 50
top / *Sheridan:* p. 41, p. 47, p. 48 bottom and center, p. 49,
p. 50 bottom left and right, p. 51 / *Stierlin:* p. 44, p. 45 top
left and right, p. 45 bottom right, p. 46, p. 48 top, p. 52, p.
57, pp. 60–64, p. 65 top left, center, bottom left and right, p.
66 top, pp. 67–68 / *Titus:* p. 77 top, p. 79 bottom, p. 83 top
right, p. 87 left, p. 89 top left and right / *Tomsich:* p. 45
bottom left.

© 1977 Rizzoli Editore-International Division
Copyright © 1979 by HBJ Press, Inc.

Library of Congress Catalog Card Number: 78-19642
ISBN: 0–15–003733–3

Printed in Italy

Coordinator, Vilma Maggioni

Editorial Supervisor, Gianfranco Malafarina

Research Organizer, Germano Facetti

U.S. Edition Coordinator, Natalie Danesi
  Murray

Contents

Preface

The Closed Faith

Jesus said, "My kingdom is not of this world."

Many of Christ's followers have made these words the basis of their worship, retiring from the world to concentrate on their faith. The practice of retreating from the distractions of society is, of course, not limited to Christians. Individuals of diverse faiths have traditionally sought the contemplative life, one that values the spiritual over the material. Although those called to a life of contemplation care little for material possessions, their houses of worship are often highly valued by those who live in the world. Many monasteries, for example, are repositories of sculpture, painting, and other art treasures. But places of worship also have a mystical significance which transcends religion. They speak to all faiths of an age-old question—what it means to be mortal.

One of the most private communities of the faithful is that of Mount Athos in northern Greece. On this peninsula, washed by the Aegean Sea, stands a score of monasteries, the earliest of which dates back to the tenth century. This little community, a semiautonomous theocratic republic under Greek sovereignty, is governed by a council made up of one representative from each monastery. Originally populated by hermits, Athos eventually became a thriving spiritual center of Eastern Orthodoxy, attracting vast numbers of monks not only from Greece and Serbia but also from Bulgaria and Russia. They came in search of a life of contemplation, away from the corrupt-

ing influence of society. At one time there were as many as 10,000 holy men living the communal life of the monasteries at Athos. Today there are 1,500—at most. And there are no women at all. Women are prohibited from visiting Mount Athos by edict, says the legend, of the Virgin Mary herself.

The monks of Athos are wary of anything that may distract them from their principal task, the worship of God. For this reason, the community has never been a center of learning or intellectual activity. During its early years even the study of the Scriptures was discouraged. Yet the monasteries are repositories of priceless icons, reliquaries, and manuscripts, as well as beautiful fourteenth-century Macedonian frescoes.

Today the rigors of life at Mount Athos do not attract many recruits. But the monks who live there do not care to justify themselves in the world's terms. Apparently unconcerned about the future of their community, they continue their lives of prayer and fasting without distractions from the outside world.

Despite their isolation, however, such closed communities often exhibit a firm national loyalty during times of trouble. In the Greek War of Independence, Mount Athos was occupied by 3,000 Turkish troops because of its Nationalist loyalties. Similarly, the monastery in the Rila Planina mountain range in Bulgaria became a stronghold of that nation's cultural heritage throughout the long years of Ottoman oppression.

The Rila monastery was founded early

in the tenth century by disciples of the anchorite Saint Ivan of Rila, who retired to a cave in the Rila mountains at the age of twenty to escape the worldliness of the Bulgarian court. Drawn by his example, a monastic community of his followers established itself not far from his retreat. Rejecting the active life, they devoted themselves to prayer and daily religious services.

Over the centuries the original monastery—attacked by bandits, Moslem and Turkish invaders, and often ravaged by fires—has been all but destroyed. Today's buildings date only from the nineteenth century, yet they are a priceless monument of Bulgarian architecture. Their sheer, forbidding walls harbor countless treasures of Bulgarian art: frescoes, icons, paintings, and religious manuscripts. By virtue of its isolation, lost in the thickly wooded mountains, the Rila monastery preserved the historic and cultural traditions of the Bulgarian people and became a symbol of national pride and hope early in the nineteenth century, when Bulgaria was actively seeking its independence.

Not all Christians who devote themselves to God choose to retire completely from everyday life. Of the three orders of Franciscan friars, founded by Saint Francis of Assisi, not all even elect to live in religious communities: Some remain in the world. In fact, the Franciscans were prominent in medieval university life and have always been active missionaries following the example of Saint Francis, who gave up all his worldly possessions and physical comforts to don his drab tunic and preach the gospel.

A few years before his death, Francis received the stigmata, the wounds of the Crucifixion of Jesus Christ, and was thenceforth never free from pain. Yet Francis's poetry, like his life, is full of "joy in all created things." The church of San Francesco in Assisi, built in his honor immediately after his death, also echoes the spirit of the saint in its many-windowed, open interior and its cycles of vibrant frescoes by many of the Italian masters, including Giotto and Cimabue.

There are few religious edifices which can rival the Palatine Chapel at Aachen in West Germany in historical significance. When Charlemagne became emperor of the Western world, he chose Aachen, the town of his birth, as his northern capital. Thus Aachen became in a sense the first capital of what we now think of as Europe. Charlemagne's eighth-century palace chapel was the religious center of this vast empire.

The chapel's design imitates in many respects the impressive imperial church of San Vitale at Ravenna—thus deliberately emphasizing Charlemagne's own majesty and authority. Today the palace of Charlemagne is long gone. Its octagonal chapel remains, however, with its golden mosaics, beautiful porphyry columns, and the white marble throne of the emperor—a living monument to the Carolingian era and a tangible symbol of the emperor who lives on in countless medieval legends and *chansons de geste* as the warlike but God-fearing father of Europe.

While Charlemagne is best remembered for championing the Christian faith against the infidel, the cathedral at Monreale, near Palermo in Sicily, is evidence of the adaptability of the same religion. Today Monreale is a quiet agricultural and tourist center with a magnificent view of the lush Conca d'Oro plain, but its history is an amalgamation of cultures, a legacy as colorful as it is unique.

Sicily was invaded by the Normans early in the eleventh century. Here, as in their other conquests, the Normans proved themselves moderate and tolerant. The third Norman king of Sicily, William

the Good, began building the cathedral at Monreale in 1174, in gratitude for his military successes. A basilica with square Norman towers, the church is a magnificent combination of Romanesque, Byzantine, and Saracen architectural traditions. Among its treasures are beautiful copper doors by Bonanno Pisano and a cycle of gold mosaics in the Byzantine tradition. Notable among these is the huge figure of Christ Pantocrator, his hand raised in a gesture that casts a blessing over the half-domed ceiling of the apse. The adjacent cloisters—the remains of a Benedictine monastery—are decorated with 228 twin columns, each one differently ornamented.

Monreale is by no means the only monument built by foreigners on Italian soil. The ruined temples of Paestum, near the city of Naples in southern Italy, are evidence of the faith and art left by colonists who came from the wealthy Greek city of Sybaris in the seventh century B.C. Many left their overcrowded native city—itself a colony—to establish a home on the flat plains near the Gulf of Salerno. They called their new home Poseidonia and dedicated the city to Hera and Athena. Although the Greeks preferred to build their temples on hills or promontories, they were forced—for lack of high ground at Poseidonia—to break with tradition. They built their monuments within the city proper, relying on architecture alone to create a sense of sacred isolation.

The remains of the three travertine temples—two dedicated to Hera, one to Athena—are remarkable and rare examples of the Doric style. Despite the damage of the centuries, they still exhibit the majestic power that characterizes ancient Greek architecture. Today the venerable columns seem at once serene and melancholy, recalling a faith that has been virtually lost for thousands of years.

Architecture helps us to reclaim the past, to write or rewrite history. The discovery of Petra, the abandoned rock city in the Jordan Desert, brought to light another lost faith, the worship of the Arab deity Dusares. Until the last century, the ancient city of Petra, the capital and thriving commercial center of the Nabataeans,

was presumed to have vanished from the face of the earth. Then in 1812, the Swiss explorer John Lewis Burckhardt walked through a mile-long narrow cleft in the sandstone desert mountains and came upon the spectacular monuments hewn out of the cliffs. The public buildings of the city which filled the enclosed space between the mountains have largely disappeared, but the edifices sculpted into the cliff face are well preserved, revealing the cultural influences which met and mingled at Petra: Greek, Egyptian, Assyrian, and Roman.

The rooms are bare, almost cavelike, but because the façades are not supporting walls, they are extraordinarily elaborate and sophisticated—especially those of the magnificent "Baroque" monument known as El-Deir, which was either a temple or the tomb of an eminent citizen. Lost in the wilderness, dramatically juxtaposed against the fractured cliff face, these sculptures are temples of silence to a people and a faith which have long since passed into history.

The Cathedral of Santiago de Compostela in Galicia, a region in the northwest of Spain, is still one of the chief shrines of Christendom. During the Middle Ages, however, it was—after Jerusalem and Rome—the most famous pilgrimage site for Christians from all over Europe. In the ninth century, tradition records that the supposed tomb of Saint James was discovered by a miracle. A sanctuary was subsequently built on the site, and two centuries later the cathedral was begun. Originally Romanesque, it has since been embellished with Baroque and Plateresque additions and restorations. Its Portico de la Gloria—intricately sculpted doorways—is an early triumph of Gothic sensibility.

Santiago, with its priceless relics, still remains the special shrine of the Spanish people, whose ardent faith forms one of the cornerstones of Spanish life. In the same way, all the monuments in this volume are shrines to faiths, both living and dead. Their very existence is a tribute to our unremitting need to make sense of the world by looking beyond it.

Mount Athos

Greece

The steep, forested slopes of Athos, the Holy Mountain, in northern Greece have been a refuge for hermits and contemplatives since the early Christian era. Today, Athos is a semiautonomous theocracy of Greek Orthodox monks living in twenty monasteries and dependencies.

The monastery of Hagios Dionysiou (shown here and on the preceding page) is said to mark the spot of a fourteenth-century anchorite's vision of an "unearthly light." Its easily defended site on the eastern coast of the Athos peninsula also offered protection against pirates. The bright red katholikon, or principal church (just visible above), stands at the center of Dionysiou's fortresslike complex. Most of the buildings date from the sixteenth century, with the exception of the modern, concrete-piered addition (left foreground above).

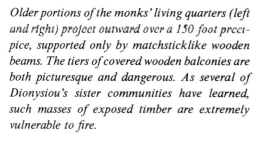

Older portions of the monks' living quarters (left and right) project outward over a 150 foot precipice, supported only by matchsticklike wooden beams. The tiers of covered wooden balconies are both picturesque and dangerous. As several of Dionysiou's sister communities have learned, such masses of exposed timber are extremely vulnerable to fire.

The great keep of Dionysiou (left) houses the monastery's library and other treasures. Typically, the keep of a Mount Athos monastery—Athonite communities always have at least one such fortified tower—is the tallest and strongest structure and dominates the rest of the complex. Below left, an inscription set high up in the wall of the keep.

In general, the monastery's layout consists of a rectangular compound of buildings, often protected by corner towers. Within the central courtyard stand the religious buildings which usually include the katholikon and the trapeza, or refectory.

The plan of the trapeza (facing page) resembles a Latin church and is furnished with an apse as well as a raised pulpit for mealtime scripture readings. Dionysiou is one of eleven monasteries that still follow the Rule of St. Basil, which calls for communal dining. The monks consume their frugal, vegetarian meals in silence before life-sized portraits of Athonite holy men. The frescoes, executed in 1603, also depict scenes from the life of Christ.

This detail (left) from the frescoes of the Diony-siou refectory shows Christ enthroned amidst a choir of angels. Beneath them, Lucifer and his followers plunge into hell. Another fresco cycle in the refectory cloister depicts scenes of the Last Judgment: The Abysmal Furnace *(top right), described in the ninth chapter of Revelations, spews forth locusts with human faces and scorpi-onlike stings to torture nonbelievers. Center right, the bodies of* The Saved. *Bottom right, three of the* Four Knights of the Apocalypse. *Their faces were scratched out by Moslem Turk-ish troops in the early nineteenth century. Above, the ornately carved doors in the Diony-siou trapeza which lead to the cloister.*

Looming 800 feet above the Aegean Sea, the cliff-top monastery of Simon Petra, founded in 1363, is the most dramatic sight on Athos. It is best known for the dizzying tiers of wooden balconies that hang suspended from the seaward façade (left). Though the balconies appear quite old, the monastery's buildings have been gutted several times by fires. The most recent reconstruction was in 1892.

Visitors to Simon Petra face a steep climb along a narrow stone staircase that zigzags up the side of the cliff and ends in an arched passageway (near right). An aqueduct (above right and detail far right) carries water from the mountain to the community.

The monastery of Saint Paul was established by Serbians and Bulgarians in the fifteenth century and is thus one of the younger communities on Athos. A crenelated wall (above) that protects the enclosure from outsiders was raised in 1522, but the monks' living quarters were rebuilt after a major fire early in this century. Saint Paul's katholikon was erected in 1844 and is rather plain by Athonite standards. Its many-domed cupolas (left) follow a traditional Byzantine pattern. The floor plan of the church typically follows the shape of a Greek cross (right), which is obscured by the addition of extra chapels, a substantial narthex, and the liti, or narthex porch.

Following page, one of the Holy Mountain's subsidiary monasteries, or sketes. Under the Byzantine Empire, Athos was inhabited by more than 10,000 monks. Sketes like this offered a more secluded alternative to the bustling, regimented daily routines of the greater monastic establishments.

The Great Laura (above), begun in 963, is the oldest monastery on Athos. A carved panel (left) recalls how the founder, Saint Athanasius, received his charge from the Virgin Mary, who smote a rock to create a spring on the site. No fewer than fifteen small churches and shrines crowd the central courtyard (top right). The early sixteenth-century refectory (center right) is considered to be the finest on Athos, containing many well-preserved frescoes. Every Athonite monastery has its phiale, or sacred well, which is sometimes simply a vessel filled with holy water. The phiale of the Great Laura (right) is possibly the best example of its kind. Its sixteenth-century porphyry basin is enclosed in a brick pavilion, and sculpted marble slabs at the base of the pavilion columns date from the monastery's founding in the tenth century.

A pair of cypress trees, which symbolize eternal life, traditionally flanks the phiales on Athos. Those at the Chilandari monastery (left) dominate the main courtyard. The Serbian King Stephen Nemanja founded Chilandari (below right) in 1197. In more recent times, it has been occupied chiefly by Bulgarians. Above, seraphs in bas-relief on one of the arcades of the inner courtyard.

The ornate trapeza cloister at Chilandari (right), with its patterned cobblestone paving, was built in the eighteenth century. The dining room within is seldom used. Chilandari is an idiorrythmic, or decentralized, monastery, and the monks take their meals in private apartments.

The elaborately patterned brick and stone masonry of the monastic buildings (below) is characteristic of late thirteenth-century Byzantine architecture. The decorated doors reflect a Serbian influence.

Vatopedi, the largest and richest of the peninsula's communities, also prides itself on being the most innovative. Its towering keep holds an extensive library collection that includes 634 Greek manuscripts and 150 ancient musical scores as well as a copy of Ptolemy's Geography. Vatopedi follows the less austere idiorrythmic rule, and it alone has adopted the modern system of telling time. The clock tower, which abuts the red porch of the katholikon (above left), and the nearby bell tower both date from 1427. They are the oldest structures of their kind on Athos. Some Athonite monks still regard church bells as a foreign novelty.

The lavish use of color (left) is unique to Vatopedi. Bright red, which is also the color of several of the katholikons, symbolizes the blood of Christ.

Vatopedi's phiale is unusually elaborate, having a frescoed central dome (above right) supported and surrounded by a central double circle of columns (below right).

A number of the twenty ruling monasteries on Mount Athos are built close to the sea. Pantocrator (top left) has occupied this small peninsula since 1357. Esphigómenou (center left), now solid and prosperous looking, played a negligible role in Athonite history until the last century. It had close ties, however, with Russia. In an attempt to gain control of this strategic territory, the czarist regime began to flood the community with novices in the mid-nineteenth century. The present buildings date from that era. Xenophontos (bottom left) has been reconstructed at least four times since the eleventh century. Its beach-side location may reflect the maritime interests of its sponsor, Stephen the Eunuch, who was an admiral in the Byzantine navy before he retired to a monk's cell here.

The capital of the Holy Republic of Mount Athos is the village of Kariai. Here stands the Protaton (above right), the foremost and oldest church on Athos. The tenth-century Protaton has undergone many restorations and is unusual among Byzantine churches for having a timber roof instead of the customary dome.

The Protaton's fourteenth-century frescoes by Michael Panselenus (below near right) are of special interest to scholars. Although damaged by age and dampness, they have escaped the frequent restorations that mar most of the monastery paintings.

The winding main street of Kariai (center and bottom far right) is lined with a few inns, the governor's house, and a handful of shops kept by monks selling "pious souvenirs" (woodcarvings and small icons) to the occasional visitor.

Sunset over Athos (following page), when the monastery gates are shut tight against the world, is still the most important time in a monk's daily routine of prayer and meditation. Today, with a population that has dwindled to a small community of elderly monks, Athos seems to have reached the twilight of its long history as the largest religious settlement on earth.

Mount Athos Greece

Traditionally, monasteries have been not so much retreats from the outside world as complete worlds in and of themselves. In medieval Europe or Buddhist Tibet, prayer was an important vocation, and the young man who felt called to a life of contemplation could become part of a thriving community with its own traditions, rules, and hierarchy. Today, as the American writer Thomas Merton—a monk himself—has pointed out, a monastic calling is more likely to be regarded as "a problem and a scandal."

Those places where monasticism still survives, such as at Mount Athos, provide some of our only insights into this once widespread way of life. Athos is not just one monastery but a semiautonomous theocratic republic on the Holy Mountain

of Athos. The rock-bound slopes of this Greek mountain, which occupies a peninsula on the Aegean coastline, were at one time the spiritual stronghold of Orthodox Christianity. Once a community of 10,000 monks, Athos is now inhabited by only about 1,500 aging men whose beards and thinning hair—tied up in untidy buns—long ago turned gray. In some monasteries, fewer than a score of these devotees remain.

Today, Athos is generally regarded as an oddity, a displaced fragment of the past. Most of its inhabitants do not even seem to acknowledge the existence of time itself—let alone accept the modern world's mechanical way of measuring it. In a typical Athonite monastery the moment of sunset, whenever it occurs, is counted as twelve o'clock and the beginning of a new calendar day. As the length of each day differs from its predecessor, timepieces must be reset daily throughout the year. Nevertheless, this is how time was reckoned under the Byzantine Empire, and only the monastery of Vatopedi, a community which prides itself on being "innovative," has ever bothered to switch to a system more compatible with mechanical timekeeping.

No doubt one of the greatest advan-

tages of this bizarre approach to telling time is its disorienting effect on visitors. The monks of Athos do not welcome the merely curious, and anyone who wishes to visit the communities for some religious or scholarly purpose must apply for a special permit, issued by the governing body of Orthodox monks. After submitting references and securing a pass, the applicant must register again with the Greek civil police.

Once on Athos, the visitor becomes a guest of the monks, who provide food and accommodations which, while not luxurious, are often superior to what the monks themselves enjoy. In return for this hospitality, the guest's behavior may be closely regulated. For example, tape recorders and movie cameras are forbidden. Not too many years ago, a startled layman was even scolded for immodestly removing all his clothes inside a bathhouse.

No women are allowed to visit Athos. Technically, this prohibition applies to females of any species. However, the rule is relaxed when applied to keeping hens and pet cats. Aside from these rare exceptions, Athos is still the most exclusively male society on earth. One monk, Michael Tolotus, who is said to have been brought to Athos as an orphan only four hours old,

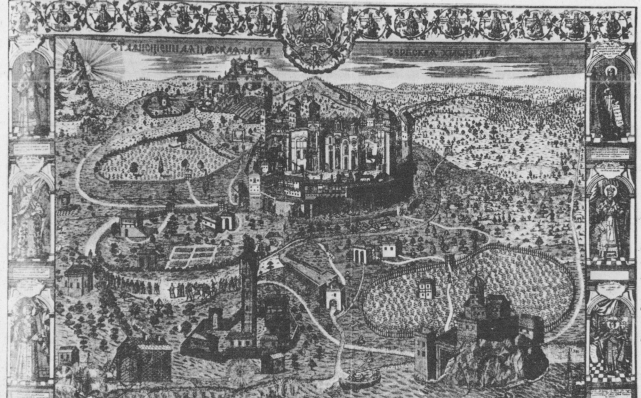

Above, Constantine the Great who made Christianity a lawful religion throughout the Roman Empire in the fourth century. Tradition says that the first hermits came to the Holy Mountain of Athos during his reign. Left, an early engraving of the Chilandari monastery on Athos.

Above left, the ascetic life of Peter-the Hermit, the first saint of Athos, as depicted in an eleventh-century miniature. The Emperor John Comenus (above right) was patron saint of several monasteries between 1118 and 1143.

Below left, the Byzantine general Nicephorus II Phocas, bestowing privileges on the Great Laura, the first large monastery on Athos; below center, the patriarch Jeremiah dedicating the Stavronikita monastery to Saint Nicholas; and below right, Emperor John Tzimisces presenting the Great Laura to God.

died during World War II without ever setting eyes on a woman.

Ironically, the monks of Athos maintain that this rule against women was promulgated by the Virgin Mary herself. An old legend relates that during the first century Jesus' friend Lazarus, having become the bishop of Cyprus, invited the then elderly Mary to pay him a visit. En route, Mary's ship was caught in a storm and forced ashore at Athos. Her arrival caused a great uproar among the pagan statues of the coastal town. All of the idols suddenly came to life and shouted, "Look, here comes the Mother of God! Hasten to honor her." Then, attempting to follow their own command, they flung themselves to the ground and shattered into thousands of pieces. At this point, the townspeople requested baptism and converted their temple of Apollo into a Christian monastery.

With this, Mary's presence became so firmly established on Athos that it ultimately led to the exclusion of all other women from the peninsula. In the fifth century B.C., the Byzantine Empress Pulcheria is said to have tried to bring some gifts to a group of monks living at the site of what is now Vatopedi. The empress was restrained, however, when a statue of the Virgin commanded, "Go no farther; in this place there is another queen than thou." In the fifteenth century, Princess Mara, widow of the Ottoman Sultan Murad II, was similarly turned away by a vision when she brought the gold, frankincense, and myrrh of the Three Magi to Athos for safekeeping.

As historians have observed, the Virgin Mary's behavior toward these well-meaning women does not appear to have been particularly Christian. There has even been some speculation that the stories were originally related to some pagan goddess of a local cult.

In fact, there are just as many pagan as

Christian legends about the Holy Mountain of Athos. For instance, the 6,667-foot mountain is named after an illegitimate son of the sea god Poseidon who, in the midst of a family quarrel, picked it up from its original location in Thrace and angrily flung it to its present site. It is not difficult to see why the people of Classical times connected Athos with Poseidon. The long, narrow spit of land where Mount Athos stands combines with two sister peninsulas to create a shape very much like the sea god's trident.

The early inhabitants of Athos, who moved onto the peninsula from the mainland to the north, appear to have been torn in their allegiance between their old god Zeus and the demands of the native deity, Poseidon. Jealous rumblings overhead encouraged Athonite loyalties to remain with Zeus, and Poseidon never forgave them. This neatly explains the treacherous currents and nasty squalls that have made the sea near Athos notorious among sailors. The Persian Emperor Darius is said to have lost a fleet of 300 trireme warships in those waters. To avoid a repetition of this disaster, his son Xerxes built a canal across the peninsula, supposedly wide enough to allow two triremes to pass through it abreast. Traces of this work, attributed to the Persian engineer Bubares, who died in 481 B.C., are still visible today. Later, Arcadius, son of the Byzantine Emperor Theodosius the Great, would have lost his life in the roiling seas around Athos had not the Virgin herself plucked him from the depths and deposited him safely in a bramble bush.

In the early centuries of the Christian era, the very inaccessibility of Athos made it attractive to holy men who wanted to escape the corrupting influence of society. Unfortunately, little more than legend is recorded of this period. The history of Athos is not that of monasteries, but of hermits who, like their patron Saint Anthony, rejected every aspect of human society and sought salvation through continual prayer and extreme asceticism. Typical of these recluses was the ninth-century Saint Peter the Athonite, who lived for

thirty-five years in a cave, eating only herbs and "manna." Another hermit, Saint Euthymius, spent forty days living like a wild beast, walking on all fours and eating grass. Later, he retired to a vermin-infested cave for three years. Upon emerging—for unknown reasons—Euthymius found to his horror that his piety had attracted a circle of admiring disciples. Disgusted, he retired once more, this time to the top of a tall pillar.

Even though the hermits' legal claim to the Holy Mountain had been recognized by Constantinople, groups of monks persisted in settling around the retreats of the more illustrious mystics, forming small communal villages known as *lauras.* Such monks were the spiritual descendants of two fourth-century monks, Saint Pacho-

The anchorite Saint Euthymius (above left), who was the founder of the first great Athonite monastery, and Saint Athanasius (above center) are two of the leading figures in the Holy Mountain's history. Above, the governor Alexander and his two sons consecrate the Dochiariou monastery. Below, Saint John Chrysostom at prayer, from a fresco in the Chilandari monastery.

mius and Saint Basil. Both men shared with Saint Anthony a belief in asceticism and constant prayer, but they ultimately

Left, a watercolor of Chilandari by F. Perilla, author of a 1927 study on Athos. The drawing of John Colobus (above) is taken from a Chilandari fresco. Below, a plan of a typical monastery compound: The archontaria *are guest quarters and the "A's" denote monks' cells.*

rejected the solitary life, claiming that it was a denial of the Christian principle of brotherly love. Their teachings as codified in the Rule of St. Basil set forth a way to combine piety with a more normal daily routine. By the end of the ninth century, Athos was the home of several thriving communities which faithfully followed these precepts.

The first of the large Athonite monasteries was founded in the year 963 by Saint Athanasius. Great Laura, which survives today, was a true monastic community, not just a gathering of independent hermits. The monks shared everything, followed the rules for group living set down by Saint Basil, and subjected themselves to the authority of the abbot, or *igoumenos* as he is known in the Orthodox Church. Athanasius' patron in this enterprise was a pious Byzantine general, Nicephorus II Phocas, who had vowed to retire to Great Laura at the conclusion of a campaign against the Saracens on Cyprus. Nicephorus never kept his vow; instead, he married the beautiful but corrupt Empress Theophano, who had him murdered shortly thereafter. Athanasius, too, was

killed when a half-completed dome of his monastery church collapsed on him.

The fate of these two founders of Athonite communal monasticism might have been interpreted as a bad omen, but other groups were not discouraged. Two more communities, Iveron and Vatopedi, were begun within a few years. And during the eleventh century, ten more monasteries, eight of which still exist, were founded. The population of these communities continued to grow steadily until the fall of Constantinople in 1453, and even then there was sufficient momentum to found Stavronikita, the last of the twenty ruling monasteries, in 1540.

Unlike the great monasteries of the Roman Catholic Church, these Athonite establishments never became important centers of learning. The monks devoted themselves to contemplation and fasting, and they shared with their hermit brothers a suspicion of any form of useful activity, physical or intellectual. In the early years, even study of the scriptures was not encouraged, as it could lead to counterproductive doubts and arguments.

Despite their profound disinterest in the

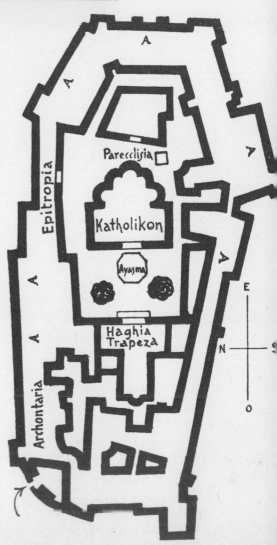

Left, a scene from the Miracle of the Two Archangels, a narrative fresco in the exonarthex of Dochiariou's katholikon. Below, the four-part seal of the Holy Republic of Mount Athos, whose autonomy is guaranteed by the Greek constitution of 1927.

itary purposes by flooding the monasteries with Russian nationals. In more recent times, new monks from Communist-controlled countries have sometimes been

outside world, the monks could not remain completely isolated. One major crisis arose in 1274 when the Emperor Michael VIII Palaeologus was forced to make a treaty that acknowledged the supremacy of Pope Gregory X. Western priests soon began to arrive on Athos, determined to spread their version of Catholicism. Martyrs were counted on both sides, but the Athonites proved more stubborn than their unwelcome guests, and by 1393, a monastery built by the Latin priests was in neglected ruin.

A second major dispute, which began on Athos and had repercussions throughout the Byzantine world, concerned the monks' practice of Hesychasm, a method of prayer that included contemplation of the navel and constant repetition of Jesus' name, rather like the chanting of a mantra. Although its practices were violently attacked after ten years of dispute, Hesychasm was accepted by the Orthodox hierarchy in Constantinople.

Oddly enough, the fall of Constantinople to the Turks brought Athos the isolation it had always sought. The new Moslem rulers were not interested in disputes

over fine points of Christian doctrine, and in exchange for a pledge of loyalty, they left the monks alone. This peace was not violated until the early nineteenth century when, quite uncharacteristically, the Athonites became involved in the War of Greek Independence (1821–1829). Without actively participating in the fighting, the monks let it be known that they favored the Nationalists, and this led to the occupation of Athos by 3,000 Turkish troops in 1821. Before the soldiers departed, the monastery of Chilandari was ransacked, and several libraries and treasures all over the peninsula were severely damaged.

Ever since this incident, politics have never quite disappeared from the Holy Mountain. The majority of the monasteries on the peninsula are inhabited by Greeks, though Serbians, Bulgarians, and Russians also have their own communities, which grew rapidly during the last two centuries.

In the nineteenth century, this expansion led the governing monks to accuse czarist Russia of attempting to take over the strategically located peninsula for mil-

suspected of being infiltrators—which is particularly unfortunate as they form the only substantial pool of potential recruits for the fast-emptying monasteries.

While the fall of the Byzantine Empire had little direct impact on the independence of Athos, the subsequent loss of financial patronage did change the character of its religious life. Inevitably, the large communal monasteries suffered most. Increasingly, the monks had to meet their own expenses, and in return, they demanded more freedom from the authority of the abbot.

In time, many of the monasteries abandoned the Rule of St. Basil and developed a new system, never very popular with the Orthodox Church, known as idiorrythmia. This practice allowed a monk to live in a private room or cell where he prepared his own food and conducted his own private devotions. A senior or more wealthy monk might even have a personal acolyte to perform cleaning or cooking chores for him. All monks were supposed to attend required prayers and observe fasts, but the abbot, who had once enforced such disciplines, was replaced by a three-man governing board that had far less authority. And, with the exception of great feast days, the elaborately decorated refectories, where all the monks gathered for meals and daily devotions, stood empty.

The ruling monasteries, whether communal or idiorrythmic, exercised control over the whole Athonite peninsula through their ownership of the land and membership in the governing council, or Epistasia. But Athos, which at one time was estimated to have had more than 10,000 residents, never ceased to attract solitary holy men and less organized communities. Although today the population of the peninsula has fallen off to less than 1,500, the skeleton of the complex organization which once held all these groups

Above, Mohammed II, conqueror of Constantinople. Athos submitted to Turkish rule under his father, Murad II, in 1430. Right, a watercolor of the Simon Petra monastery.

together still survives.

The major monasteries had several types of subsidiaries. One of these was the *skete*, a kind of monastic colony. Some sketes were quite grand and differed from their mother houses only in that they rented the land they occupied and had no representation on the Epistasia. Others were haphazardly organized village compounds. A lesser kind of subsidiary, lacking even the central church found in a skete, was the *kelli*. This was a simple hermitage, consisting of a few rough huts and a chapel.

Of course, there have always been ascetics who rejected any form of group living. Scattered over the peninsula in remote caves and grottoes, a handful of hermits subject themselves to the extremes of hunger and cold. Half-starved and, by any rational standard, half-mad, these men have no contact with humanity except for a monthly basket of provisions lowered into their retreats by sympathetic brothers. No attempt is ever made to communicate with a hermit; only if he fails to accept a food basket will someone climb down into the cave to see if he is still alive. When a hermit does succumb, there is usually an eager candidate waiting to occupy his cave. Later, the skull of the deceased hermit takes its place along with those of his predecessors on a shelf in the cave.

The capital of the "Republic" of the Holy Mountain is Kariai, a small village located in the center of the peninsula. Except for the absence of motor vehicles, Kariai resembles an ordinary Greek town. However, such profane pleasures as playing music, smoking, and even whistling are strictly forbidden. The twenty appointed members of the governing council, or Holy Community, live in Kariai, as does the Protos, the premier monk of Athos. His home church, the Protaton, is the oldest on the peninsula and has custody of the most sacred icon on Athos—a representation of the Virgin known as *Axion Estin*, or "Worthy It Is."

Because the terrain of the peninsula is so rugged, nearly all the ruling monasteries and sketes are ranged along the steep coastal cliffs, where they can be easily reached by boat. The monastery buildings are an anthology of Byzantine architecture. Outwardly, most of the monasteries conform to the same basic plan. They are walled structures, as close to being rectangular as the terrain will allow. The walls are sometimes reinforced by one or more towers, and there is always a central tower which holds a *semandron*, a large plank of wood that the monks carry in procession around the interior courtyard. The rapping of the semandron is supposed to symbolize Noah's calling of the birds and beasts to join him on the ark. The towers do not generally contain church bells, an "innovation" that has never taken hold on Athos.

In the center of the monastery courtyard stands the main church, or *katholikon*. This is traditionally built in the form of a Greek cross, with four arms of equal length; however, the addition of many small chapels between the arms and of apses at the ends of the arms sometimes makes the basic configuration difficult to see. A cupola tops each of the four arms of the katholikon and a larger fifth one crowns their intersection. The narthex, a covered vestibule at the front of the church, is another typically Byzantine feature, and some of the katholikons have an additional outer narthex, called a *liti*— originally, an open-air porch, but now often glassed in.

Although the monasteries of today are lonely places, their compact ground plans suggest that life for the once-numerous Athonite monks must have been far from solitary. The courtyard around the katholikon is often crowded with small shrines and chapels, many built into the church itself. The monks' cells and guest rooms are ranged around the sides of the rectangle in buildings that may be up to six stories high. Aside from the katholikon, the largest interior spaces in the monastery are those of the *trapeza,* or refectory, which curiously is like a Western church in that it is usually built in the shape of a

Latin cross, with an apse at the eastern end. The meals taken in the refectory were more likely to satisfy the soul than the stomach. Inside these elaborately painted and decorated halls the brothers ate their vegetarian meals without speaking and listened to scripture readings. The fare was, and still is, the plainest imaginable. In addition to avoiding meat, fish, and

Left, a monk sounding a semandron *as depicted in an Athonite manuscript. Below, three more versions of this ancient monastic instrument, some of which are used during religious processions: (1) one fashioned of iron (2) a portable version of wood and (3) a larger, stationary type, also of wood.*

Below, the Apocalypse, a favorite theme, on the wall of the Xerophon refectory. Below right, The Lamb of God Worshiping at his Father's Throne *found in the trapeza of the Dionysiou monastery.*

dairy products (which are believed to stimulate carnal desires), the monks normally do without olive oil, a staple of Greek cooking, because they believe that it might make them lazy.

Though it is not always obvious to the modern visitor, the Republic of the Holy Mountain is quite wealthy. The land alone—nearly one hundred square miles of wooded mountainside—is immensely valuable. Some of the monasteries do manage a thriving business in timber exports, but most make only a minimal attempt to exploit their landholdings.

The monasteries are also the repositories of artistic and historical treasures, from fourteenth-century Macedonian frescoes to large collections of smaller objects, including reliquaries, icons, and manuscripts. The Philotheou monastery, for example, owns the *Panaghia Glykophilousa,* a representation of the Virgin which, although the monks attribute it to Saint Luke, is at least a rare survival of the iconoclastic destructions of the eighth century. The traditional Iveron monastery also possesses a pre-eighth-century icon, the *Panaghia Portraitissa,* or Virgin of the

Gate, which is said to have escaped the iconoclasts by miraculously transporting itself across the sea from Constantinople to Athos. The premier treasure of the Great Laura of Saint Athanasius is a Bible donated by the monastery's original patron, Nicephorus Phocas. The otherwise poor community of Xeropotamou owns the Cup of Pulcheria, a true masterpiece in carved ophite, decorated with miniature reliefs of the Virgin.

The Holy Men of Athos, however, are largely indifferent to the monetary or aesthetic value of these objects. Instead, they lavish far more attention on such relics as purported fragments of the true cross and the "Virgin's girdle." For the most part, the art treasures of Athos are uncatalogued, seldom shown to visitors, and often poorly preserved.

The Republic of the Holy Mountain, in decline for decades now, is more desolate today than it has ever been. The Cold War has cut off the influx of Serbians, Bulgarians, and Russians which in the last century had become so important to maintaining the population of Athos. And in the West, asceticism and celibacy are no longer in fashion, to say the least. Even dedicated

young priests tend to regard the Athonites as superstition-bound misogynists. Owing to recent proposals to turn Athos over to agricultural development, charitable foundations, or even casino builders, the Orthodox Church is understandably reluctant to give out current population statistics on the communities.

Perhaps the individuals who are least concerned about the fate of Athos are the elderly monks themselves. The monastic communities have never placed any value on good works or the opinion of the secular world, and they have certainly made no effort to modernize their ways to attract new converts. At a time when too few newcomers are arriving, the Athonite monks still consider the ritualistic closing of their fortified gates at sunset the most important moment of the day. And Athonites continue to tell time by a system that defies the logic of modern timepieces. Adapting to the present and worrying about the future have never been part of the monks' vocation. They fill their hours with prayer and trust God to justify Athos to the world.

King George I of Greece (above) reclaimed Athos from the Turks in 1913. The patriarchs (left) of Mount Athos met at Kariai in 1963 to celebrate the millennium of the first communal monastery at Athos.

Paestum

Italy

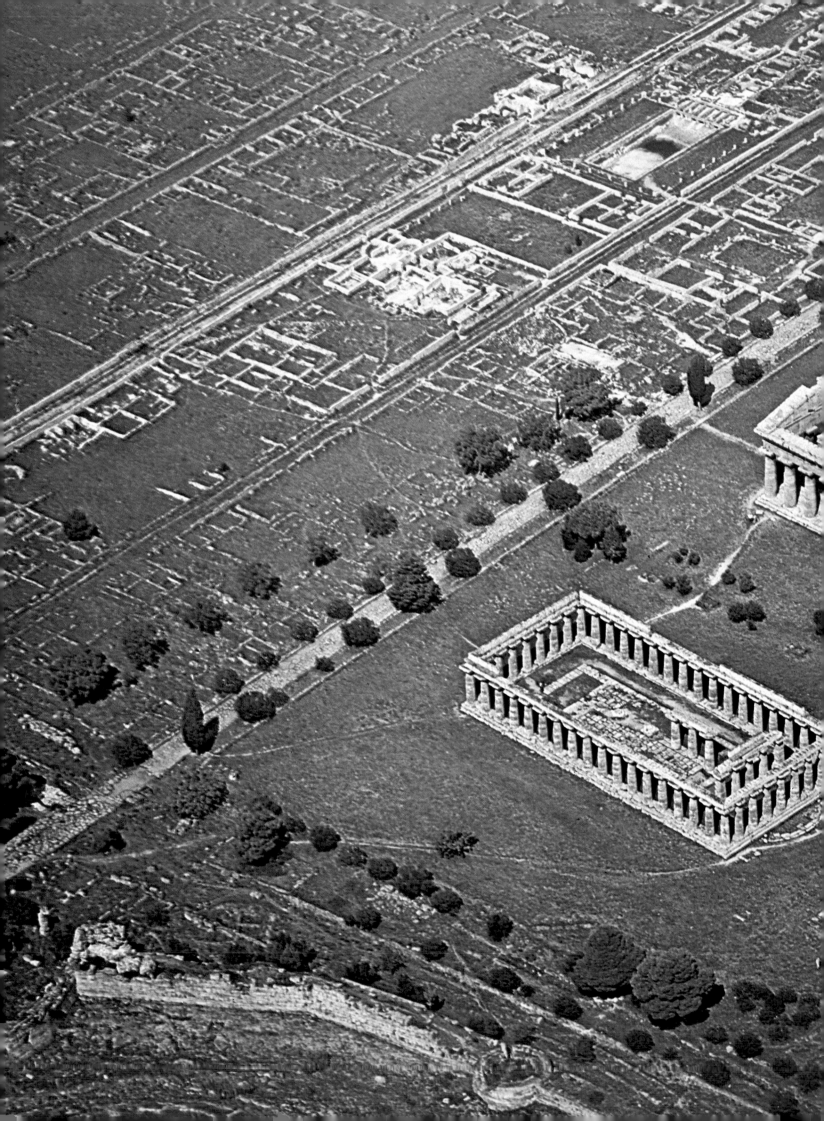

Three ancient temples are among the sole remaining monuments of the once-thriving Greek city of Poseidonia (renamed Paestum by its Roman conquerors in 273 B.C.) in southern Italy. Its two temples to Hera (preceding page: Hera I, left; Hera II, right) and another to Athena honored the patron goddesses of the city. Built in the sixth and fifth centuries before Christ, they are recognized today as some of the finest surviving examples of early Doric architecture.

The Greeks purposely imbued their temples with both human and divine qualities to better symbolically link them with their remarkably human divinities. For example, the stout columns of Hera I (these pages) thrust from the ground to the sky like human limbs straining under tremendous weight. At the same time, the strict geometric precision of the temple represents divine perfection.

When the ruins at Paestum were first discovered, they were thought to date from later Hellenistic times. The heavy, bulging columns and flattened capitals contributed to the belief that the temples were overly sophisticated and "Baroque" as compared to other known Classical Greek temples. Once it was determined that they were actually constructed during the Archaic period, admiration for the temples grew.

Hera II (these pages) is a monument of harmonious proportions and elegant balance. The vertical lines of the fluted columns and the horizontal emphasis of the entablature exemplify the simple linearity of the Doric order. The technical expertise of the early Greeks is illustrated by the solidity of the Paestum temples, whose huge travertine blocks were assembled without mortar. The columns of Hera II have a diameter of over six feet at the base and not quite five feet at the top, and have twenty-four flutings.

The discovery of hundreds of statues and vases depicting the goddess Hera indicates that her temples held a central position in the life of Paestum. Situated on a rocky eminence, Hera's two temples occupied a sacred precinct at the city's center.

Few of the residents of Paestum would have been permitted to enter the sanctuary, or cella, of Hera II (left), which housed the revered statue of the goddess. The cella was divided into three spaces by two rows of double-tiered columns that supported the flat ceiling and wooden-trussed roof of the temple.

Paestum's temple dedicated to Athena (facing page) is on slightly higher ground to the north of Hera's temples. Its fragmentary pediment hints at the weighty proportions of the original temple. Athena's temple is the first to be visible from the Gulf of Salerno, a warning to invaders of the power of Paestum's patron deity.

The Sacred Way (above) runs north to south connecting Hera I and II with the temple to Athena (in the background). This road intersected another of Paestum's main streets at the Greek agora, or marketplace, which became the site for the Romans' forum (above far right). The ruins of sacred and civic Roman buildings can still be seen along the Sacred Way.

The Romans brought wealth and new building techniques to Paestum. Characteristically, they erected gymnasiums, baths, and an amphitheater (below, left and right) that is located at the eastern end of the forum.

Below right, an older Greek "theater"—its precise use has not been determined—which was partially cut into by later Roman construction. Below, a sculpted entablature found on a Roman temple near the forum.

Following page, the columns of Hera I. The once-precise fluting counteracts the almost humanlike heaviness of the columns.

Paestum Italy

The ancient Greeks worshiped the goddess Hera, the sister-wife of Zeus, as the queen of the gods. She was the special protectress of women, presiding over all phases of feminine existence, especially marriage and childbirth. Although she was most often portrayed in Greek literature as a shrewish wife jealously spying on her husband's infidelities, her emblem was the pomegranate, symbol of conjugal love and fruitfulness. Many temples were built in her honor throughout ancient Greece, and when Greek cities founded new colonies, they established the cult of Hera on foreign soil.

About forty-five miles south of Pompeii, two Doric temples dedicated to Hera mark the site of one such colony, now known as Paestum. This ancient city near the Gulf of Salerno was founded in the seventh century B.C. by the city of Sybaris, a Greek colony farther to the south in Italy. Its first inhabitants called the new city Poseidonia after Poseidon, god of the sea. Paestum's two temples to Hera and a later one dedi-

cated to Athena stand on a wide coastal plain near the mouth of the River Sele, known to the Greeks as the Silaris, which irrigates a fertile valley about five miles north of Paestum.

Hera's two temples were built a century apart. The older temple, now simply called Hera I, dates from around 530 B.C. and was erroneously classified as a basilica by eighteenth-century archaeologists. The later temple, Hera II, was correctly identified as belonging to the city's chief deity—but the wrong one. It was assumed that Paestum's namesake Poseidon was the ranking divinity. However, excavations at the temple sites and other areas in and around the city have uncovered numerous terra-cotta statuettes representing Hera, as well as nuptial vases and other offerings to the goddess from young brides. Inscriptions on these votive vases strongly suggest that Hera was the most

important divinity of the land.

The third major surviving Doric temple at Paestum, honoring the goddess Athena, was built near the northern edge of the city in about 510 B.C. Athena, the goddess of war and victory, was also the protectress of cities. Moreover, she was the goddess of agriculture and was said to have invented the plow and given mortals the prized olive. Recent excavations of vases and statues dedicated to Athena indicate that she was overshadowed by Hera, whose cult undoubtedly had a stronger following at Paestum.

The Greek colony of Poseidonia prospered during its first few centuries. The land was fertile and the people actively engaged in building, agriculture, and worship of the gods. During the sixth and fifth centuries B.C., it was an important trading link between the Greeks and Etruscans.

Right, the plans of the three Doric temples: Hera I (top), Hera II (center), and Athena (bottom).

Charles III of Bourbon (left), who was King of Spain, Naples, and Sicily, commissioned a road to be built from Salerno to Vallo di Lucania, which made the temples at Paestum easily accessible.

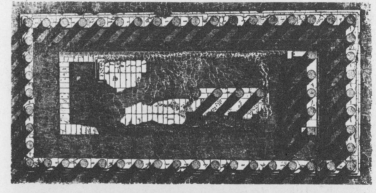

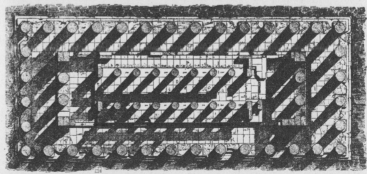

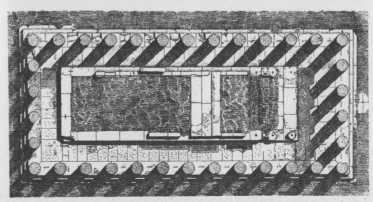

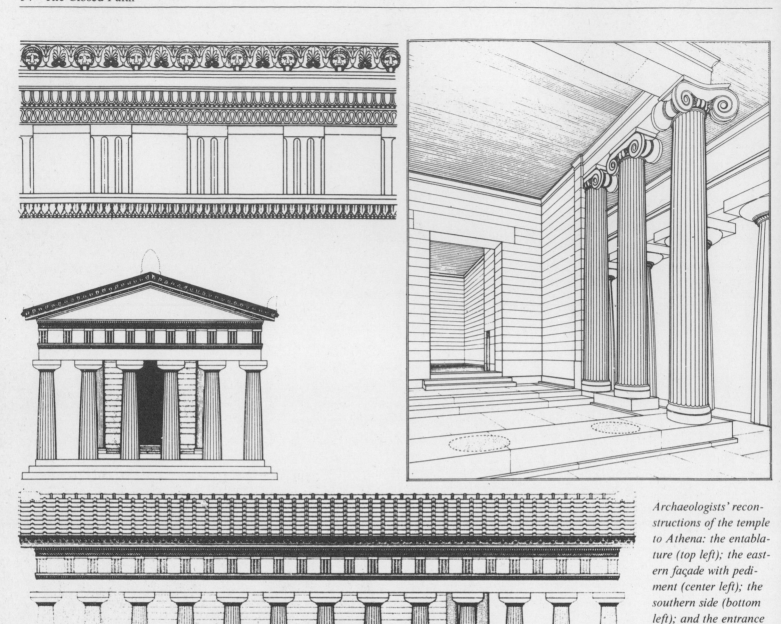

Archaeologists' reconstructions of the temple to Athena: the entablature (top left); the eastern façade with pediment (center left); the southern side (bottom left); and the entrance to the cella (above).

But when the Etruscans suffered a naval defeat in 474 B.C., Poseidonia—feeling obliged to enclose itself within a nearly three-mile-long wall—began to decline in prosperity.

Despite its defenses, the city fell to the warlike Lucanians, an Italic tribe living inland up in the hills, around 400 B.C. Disliking all things Greek, the Lucanians changed the city's name to Paiston and even forbade the use of the Greek language. Lucanian supremacy was finally eclipsed in 273 B.C., when Roman forces conquered the city. The Romans renamed the city Paestum and made it their own colony. In reward for its loyalty to Rome,

the city received several privileges, including some degree of autonomy and permission to mint its own coins. Paestum again flourished, becoming a center of trade in cereals and oils. The Romans added to the architectural wealth of the city by building baths, temples, an amphitheater, and a colonnaded forum.

Like the Lucanians before them, the Romans repaired and augmented the city's original fortifications and buildings. Archaeologists have discovered Greek foundations under a number of Roman buildings. A now partially excavated moat runs beneath the ruins of bridges serving the four tower gates situated at the com-

pass points. Moat, gates, and bridges appear to have been first built by the original Greek colonists. The most striking of the great gates is the Porta Marina facing the western sea. The Romans' forum was built on the same site and with the same east-west orientation as the Greek agora. The Romans used building elements—columns, capitals, often mismatched—from the agora to build a portico around the north, west, and south sides of the forum.

The life of Paestum revived under Roman rule. The scattered stones of the forum, some ruined public buildings, and a number of Roman shops are evidence of a vital city. Eventually, however, the forces of man and nature combined to all but annihilate the population. As the nearby mountains were stripped of their protective forests, soil-laden rainwater washed down through the valleys and the mouth of the river became clogged with sand, forming swamps that became breeding grounds for malarial mosquitoes. Many inhabitants of Paestum were forced to flee, and in time, the city was virtually abandoned. The few remaining citizens eventually fled to the mountains when the area fell prey to Saracen raiders in the ninth century A.D.

Abandoned and forgotten, Paestum lay overrun by weeds for over 1,000 years, until in 1745 a Neapolitan architect redis-covered the ruins. Over the next few dec-ades, Paestum attracted archaeologists and architects from many countries. Dur-ing the same period, the discovery of Pompeii and Herculaneum also aroused archaeological interest, enticing a horde of dilettantes and scholars to the nearby site at Paestum.

The severity of Paestum's Doric order, so different from the more refined Classi-cism, at first disconcerted architect and expert alike. Paestum seemed unorthodox. Its columns bulged excessively; its capitals were squashed; its entablatures were heavy and unwieldy. The Doric columns even lacked bases—a characteristic which eighteenth-century architects considered primitive, if not unfinished. Goethe ex-claimed upon his first visit that the mas-sive outlines appeared "heavy, not to say frightful," although he later amended his judgment. A number of years passed be-fore architects recognized and admired Paestum as a superb compendium of early Doric architecture.

Like all Classical Greek temples, those at Paestum were designed to be experi-enced from outside. Conceived as part of a unity of sky, sea, and mountains, their shape was subtly influenced by their set-ting. Moreover, certain types of land-scapes were regarded by the Greeks as sa-cred to particular gods or as embodiments of their presence. The structure of the

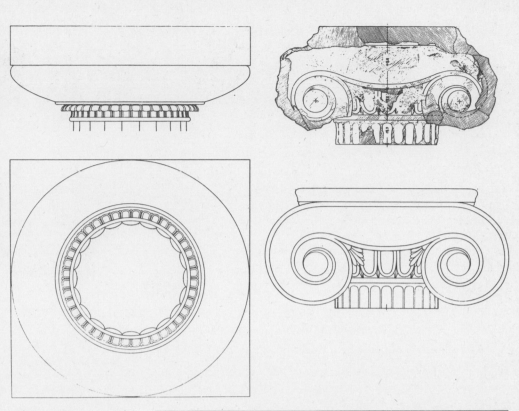

Above, a Doric capital from the temple to Athena. Top right, a "restored" Ionic capital from its cella. Right, a lion-head waterspout decorating the gutter molding.

temples and their relationship both to the landscape and to each other was intended to enhance and complement—or some-times even to contradict—the meaning that was felt in the land itself.

When building their temples, the Greeks sought a balance between the fluid, anthropomorphic architectural fea-tures expressing human aspirations and limitations and the geometric perfection and precision that evoked the divine. The severity and control of the Doric order was reinforced by a thin covering of smooth white stucco, painted with sky and earth colors of strong blues and terra-cotta reds on the friezes. The sculptures that once decorated the temples were painted in yellows, reds, browns, blues, and greens. Some were even gilded. A main thor-oughfare, the Sacred Way, kept the tem-ples distinct from the commerce of the town, yet led the people to the place of worship.

The *stereobate,* the triple-stepped base of each temple, served to elevate the sa-cred edifice above the people and to lead them toward it. The solid walls of the cellas, or enclosed inner spaces of the temples, have been destroyed, and now light floods the once-mysterious inner sanctums. To the Greeks, the temple was as much a representation of the deity as a place for sheltering the godhead.

Paestum lacked the hills or promon-tories upon which the Greeks traditionally preferred to build their temples. Faced with Paestum's flat terrain, they set the two main temples, Hera I and II, in the large *temenos,* or sacred space, at the city center. The third temple to Athena, built in a temenos to the north, was connected to it by the Sacred Way. To begin with, archaeologists thought that Hera I, the oldest temple, built in the mid-sixth cen-tury B.C., was a civic rather than religious building. Neither pediment nor altar had

yet been discovered. Moreover, the uneven number of columns in the façade—nine—and the division of the cella into two aisles differed from known Doric temples. In fact, however, they were Archaic characteristics not found in more advanced temples.

Although it faces east like most Greek temples, Hera I is somewhat atypical. The exaggerated bulging, or entasis, of the columns gives them the air of straining like human limbs under the immense pressure of the stone architrave. The flattened capitals invite the same anthropomorphic analogy. The pronounced heaviness and rigidity of the columns are offset by the sharp outlines and energy of the fluting. Such distinctive columns, which were at one time thought to be Hellenistic and decadent, later were recognized as typically Archaic.

Much of the temple has been lost, but what remains, wrought in heavy travertine, conveys an aura of awesome solemnity. Seen from the west, the temple and the hill behind it appear as one. In this way the Greeks visually stressed the relationship of the city to the earth and to its gods.

In contrast to its more ponderous predecessor, Hera II is an early expression of the mature Doric style. It is the best preserved of the three temples and exhibits a special harmony and unity: massive yet graceful; solid yet airy; weighty yet perfectly balanced.

The cella of Hera II, unlike that of Hera

The gutter molding (top right) of the Roman temple at the forum has a hole where a lion-head waterspout (above) was once attached.

Above left, painted slabs of stone depicting a banquet, which were recently found in an intact tomb dating from ca. 480 B.C.

I, lacked a central spine of columns. Instead, two rows of double-tiered columns supported the wooden-trussed beams of the temple's tiled roof. Light scarcely penetrated this inner sanctuary which held the statue of the venerated goddess. Although few of the cella walls now remain, those sections that do survive show traces of the white stucco used to make the local pitted limestone appear like marble. An altar stood before the temple. A square sacrificial *bothros,* or pit, near the altar received the remains of the sacrifices.

Hera II is a study in balance. To counter the illusion of sagging horizontal lines, both roof edge and steps bow upward very slightly—about three-quarters of an inch—while the subtly slanted corner columns correct any illusion that they bend outward. Since the six columns across the front and back are slightly larger than those that flank the temple, the corner columns are elliptical and appear to correspond in size with whichever row of columns is viewed. Such optical tricks demonstrate the surprising expertise of the Greek architects. Far from being decadent, Hera II is an example of the continued search for the perfection of the Doric temple.

The temple to Athena, built in 510 B.C., stands on higher ground than Hera I and II, assuming a symbolic protective role against invaders approaching from both land and sea. The temple columns are grouped more tightly and lean inward, increasing the impression of height and prominence. The exaggerated height of the frieze, the narrow architrave, and the lack of a horizontal cornice across the base of the pediment all enhance its vertical thrust.

The three Doric temples at Paestum were the expressions of the depth and intensity of the religious feeling of an ancient culture, which is not difficult to understand in our own time. Even today, a vestige of the cult of Hera survives—carried long ago into the mountains outside Paestum by refugees fleeing barbarians and malaria at the end of the Roman Empire. There, in the mountain village of Capaccio Vecchio, stands a church dedicated to the Madonna of the Pomegranate—with which Hera was identified. Twice a year processions file up mountain paths to the twelfth-century church carrying small votive boats that contain offerings of flowers and wax candles, much as the Greeks used to do 2,500 years before.

Petra

Jordan

Preceding page, tombs just outside the cleft in the craggy mountains that leads into the rock-hewn necropolis of Petra. This ancient desert city in Jordan was occupied by the Nabataeans at least four centuries before Christ. The ruins of Petra are often called the "rose-red city" because of the distinctive color of the rock in which they are cut. The carved façades in this exposed cliff have suffered considerable erosion, but Assyrian-style, crow's-foot step motifs are still discernible on some of them.

Above, El-Deir, the largest façade in the Petra necropolis. Far left, unique Nabataean-horned capitals and simple disks ornamenting the entablature. Near left, the urn that tops the central kiosk of El-Deir. The man sitting beneath it indicates the enormous scale of the building. The complex façade (right), which was carved out of the cliff face, would have been less easily constructed had it been built up out of quarried stone.

Below and far right, the splendid El-Khaznah al-Faroun, or so-called Treasury of the Pharaoh. Sheltered by the rock cliff from which it is carved, the façade is well preserved. The upper half of the third column from the left, however, is a replacement made in 1960. The sculptural reliefs (right) were destroyed not by the weather but by religious iconoclasts opposed to pictorial images. Above, the exquisite carving on the central kiosk of El-Khaznah. Its sophistication suggests that the architect and artisans came from a major center of Hellenistic culture.

Many architectural styles and influences are represented at Petra. Above left, the Egyptian-like Obelisk Tomb. Beneath it, but disconcertingly out of alignment, is another tomb or possibly a reception chamber for the Obelisk Tomb. Below left, the badly eroded Palace Tomb, supposedly modeled after a Roman palace. Above, a section of the Roman amphitheater. In 1962, the Jordanian government staged a special program here commemorating the 150th anniversary of the rediscovery of Petra by John Lewis Burckhardt. Above right, Assyrian-style tombs. Right, the so-called Tomb of the Roman Soldier, which may have been built for a Roman proconsul in Petra. Below, the beautifully sculpted, naturally colored room connected to the Tomb of the Roman Soldier. Below right, rectangular tombs—variations on the stone block with the proportions 4 x 2 x 1—that represented Dusares, god of fertility.

The badly eroded façade (left) of the Silk Tomb was so named because the bands of brilliantly colored sandstone look like watered silk. Bottom far right, some of the remarkable, striated rock at Petra.

Above, the Assyrian-style dwellings or tombs—it is not always clear which they were meant to be—on the so-called Street of Façades. They resemble petrified versions of the mud buildings of Mesopotamia. Top right, an isolated corner of the sacred high place on the mountain Zibb Atuf. Center right, an obelisk representing Dusares, the principal god of Petra. These sandstone steps (near right), now worn by time, were once common throughout the mountains around Petra.

Following page, the first view of El-Khaznah from the chasm leading to Petra.

Petra
Jordan

"The camel caravans crossing the country were like armies on the march." Thus the Greek geographer Strabo, writing in the first century B.C., described the traffic across the deserts of Jordan to the pink sandstone city of Petra. The caravans came from Mada' in Salih in Arabia bearing frankincense and myrrh. From Kuwait on the Persian Gulf they carried Indian spices and silks from China. From the Gulf of Aqaba they brought Nubian ivory, Egyptian gold objects, and pearls from southern Arabia. Down along the rift valley from the Dead Sea they carried bitumen and balsam from Jericho. At Petra, where so many trade routes met and crossed, the caravans stopped to exchange and supplement their cargoes with exquisite local pottery and copper wares, before heading north to Damascus or west to Gaza on the Mediterranean.

The only entrance to Petra was through a cleft in the mountains that surrounded this capital and commercial center of a people known as the Nabataeans. In single file the caravan passed through the mile-and-a-quarter-long cleft between the rocks, which gradually narrowed to an arm's span. In some places, the sheer rock sides rose 400 feet, almost closing together overhead and blocking out the thin blue ribbon of sky.

At the end of the chasm, the caravan would take a sharp turn to the left, coming in full view of a façade so huge and magnificent that later generations of Arabs came to call it El-Khaznah al-Faroun—the Treasury of the Pharaoh. A little beyond stood a vast amphitheater carved from the mountain side. The passage then opened onto a rocky oval plateau, a little more than a mile long and three-quarters of a mile wide.

This sheltered site was once home to 30,000 people. The plateau held the public buildings, shops, and dwellings of the city of Petra. Even more impressive were the temples, storehouses, and tombs carved out of the surrounding rock walls. These uniquely sculptured buildings were—and remain—a record of the diverse civilizations that met and intermingled in this desert wilderness. Assyrian, Egyptian, Hellenistic, and Roman elements were combined by the Nabataeans into a truly cosmopolitan architecture.

Today, however, Petra is a dead city. Accessible only by the same arduous route followed by the ancient caravans, its free-standing buildings have all but disappeared and only those carved from the rocks remain, their pockmarked façades ravaged by sand, wind, and man. Lost in the Jordan Desert, Petra remained unknown to the Western world for centuries, until the Swiss explorer John Lewis Burckhardt came upon the city in 1812.

The first known reference to Petra records that Antigonus, the Greek ruler of Syria, sent an expedition against the city in 312 B.C. with the aim of cutting off the

Right, an engraving by Maurice Linant, the first modern illustrator of Petra, showing a Roman arch. This arch spanned the cleft leading into Petra until it fell in the late nineteenth century.

Left, John Lewis Burckhardt, who in 1812 became the first Westerner to see Petra in nearly 600 years. He journeyed in the Middle East and North Africa disguised as a poor Bedouin merchant to avoid attracting attention. Accompanied only by a guide, he was unprepared for the ruins he found at Petra. As he later remarked: "Great must have been the opulence of a city which could dedicate such monuments to the memory of its rulers."

where Petra now stands is called Sela, meaning "rock"—just as Petra means "rock" in Greek. Archaeologists have excavated at Petra a circular, megalithic Edomite temple dating from about 1500 B.C., which was later built over by the Nabataeans. The most sacred "high place" of the Nabataean religion, atop the mountain Zibb Atuf, may also have been previously used by the Edomites, if only as a sentry post.

At the base of Zibb Atuf stands a royal cemetery dotted with squat rectangular and obelisk-shaped tombs. These are all variations on the simple stone block which symbolized Dusares, the principal god of Petra. Nonrepresentational images for divinities were common among the tribes of Arabia. The shapeless sacred black stone of Mecca no doubt began as the idol stone of a local god who has now been superceded by Allah.

One of Petra's major monuments, the Obelisk Tomb, is dominated by four massive obelisks standing on elongated, unadorned block bases. The similarity with Egyptian tomb architecture is striking. Yet both its portal and the higher central niche set between two pairs of obelisks are delicately Classical—a blend of the timeless majesty of Egypt with the sophisticated splendors of contemporary Greece.

Older than the Obelisk Tomb are many structures that reveal an Assyrian influence. The so-called Street of Façades, carved from the cliff face, consists of buildings, some of which were probably used as dwellings or as tombs. Their crow's-foot, stepped-cornice motifs are characteristic of Assyrian brick architecture. Apart from these elements, the façades are almost devoid of architectural details.

Although there are pronounced differences between the early façades reflecting Assyrian and Egyptian influences and

lucrative Petra-Gaza trade route from his rival, Ptolemy of Egypt. Antigonus' 5,000 Greek soldiers quickly took the city while its citizens were out meeting a caravan and carried off more than 500 talents of silver. When Petra's inhabitants returned, they immediately avenged themselves by pursuing the Greeks, recovering their goods, and killing all but fifty of the invaders. Clearly Petra was already a formidable city, both to provoke so great an attack and to rout such an imposing army.

The Nabataean inhabitants of Petra had originally been a nomadic people of the Arabian Desert who eked out an existence herding sheep and raiding caravans. By the sixth century B.C., great numbers of Nabataeans were moving into the kingdom of Edom, the mountainous country which extends from the Dead Sea to the Gulf of Aqaba. They became the dominant population, eventually absorbing the Edomites completely.

In the Bible, the Edomite settlement

those of the Hellenistic and Roman periods, construction methods remained essentially the same. The great rock buildings were more the work of sculptors and quarrymen than of architects and builders. Since the façades were not thin structural walls but the sculpted surfaces of a huge mass, their designers were freed from many of the usual physical constraints. Unlike conventional buildings, they were constructed from the top down, with great heaps of the soft sandstone rock being thrown downward or carried away as the surface was chiseled, carved, and smoothed. The interior spaces, little more than smooth-walled caves, were probably formed after the exterior.

Petra's wealth and power were at their height between the fourth century B.C. and the second century A.D. The city had escaped the notice of Alexander the Great as well as the successor states that emerged from his empire. Indeed, the rivalry between two of them, Seleucid Syria and Ptolemaic Egypt, worked in Petra's favor. Traders sent their wares through Petra rather than through territories contested by the two great powers. Petra retained its independence by playing one power against the other and by paying tribute to both. More often than not, Petra bought off, rather than fought off, its enemies.

Although politically independent, Petra was strongly influenced by Hellenistic Greek culture. Petra's most powerful ruler, Aretas III, who reigned from 84 to 56 B.C. over lands stretching from Damascus to the Red Sea, added Philhellen ("lover of things Greek") to his royal title. El-Khaznah al-Faroun was probably built during the pharaoh's reign. The treasury is composed of two distinct levels, the upper having a central kiosk flanked by broken pediment pavilions and crowned with an urn on a great Corinthian capital. The overall feeling of the façade is Hellenistic. The lower level is a full pedimented portico with freestanding Corinthian columns and an elaborate sculptural frieze. Relief sculptures representing gods and goddesses fill the niches—a far cry from the plain blocks of stone which constituted the more typical idols of Petra.

The wealth and independence of Hellenistic Petra are reflected in its largest surviving monument, El-Deir, which stands in an isolated spot high on a cliff northeast of the city. A temple or the tomb of a dignitary, it is 132 feet high and 154 wide. El-Deir contains a single room, measuring 33 by 38 feet. Its lower story has eight simple half-columns, the outer two of which are actually pilasters whose

Following Burckhardt's discovery, many nineteenth-century Europeans visited the ruins of Petra, among them Sir Richard Burton (above), a famous explorer, and Léon de Laborde (below right). This French noble led the first major scientific expedition to Petra in 1826, which he chronicled in a three-volume work Voyage de l'Arabie Petrée.

Left, an engraving of some of the Assyrian-style monuments in the Street of Façades.

flat surfaces and square corners more effectively terminate the façade than their fully rounded counterparts.

Above the solid lower level is the more open and "Baroque" upper story. Its effect is far more three dimensional. Projecting from a greatly recessed back wall are five freestanding elements, all tied together by the continuity of the story below upon which they stand. End pilasters and two broken pediment-topped pavilions flank a cylindrical central kiosk. The use of such a kiosk—more typically found as a freestanding element—is an innovation of Nabataean architecture, as are the simple, horned capitals of the columns and the plain circular disks in the frieze. Atop the conical roof of the kiosk is a large urn resting on a great horned capital. No other building captures the Nabataean Classical style more completely.

Just as it avoided being absorbed into the neighboring Hellenistic states, for almost two centuries Petra also remained outside the Roman Empire. In 63 B.C., the Roman general Pompey sent a force against the city, but Petra was able to appease him by offering tribute. The Emperor Augustus also sent a force against Petra, but the troops were misled into following a circuitous route to the city. The exhausted ranks who reached the city were also content to accept tribute and depart. Finally, in A.D. 106, Petra was annexed to the Roman Empire as capital of the province of Arabia Petraca.

At first, Petra flourished under the Roman occupation. On the level plateau of the city a colonnaded street was constructed, with impressive gates and arches, arcades of shops, and baths. Today these all lie in ruins, but the large Roman amphitheater remains, hewed from the mountain side just within the city.

Roman style was also reflected in the rock tombs built around the city. The badly eroded Palace Tomb—a many columned, three-storied façade—is thought to be modeled after a Roman palace, perhaps Nero's Domus Aurea (Golden House). The Tomb of the Roman Soldier is so named because the central carved figure, although badly damaged, is still recognizably clothed in Roman armor. Compared to its Hellenistic predecessors, the form of the building reflects the simpler, more forthright Classicism favored by the Romans, although the capitals are more Nabataean in character. The space within, which was used for Roman funeral feasts, is the only extensively carved interior in Petra.

Petra was too far from the main centers of the empire to be more than an outpost. The administrative capital of the province was transferred to Bozrah in Syria, while Palmyra, also in Syria, replaced Petra as the area's commercial center. Petra went into a decline that was only briefly stemmed in the fourth and fifth centuries when it served as the seat of a Byzantine bishopric, and several of the rock buildings were used as churches or as monks' cells. By the time Islam swept across the area in the seventh century, Petra was more or less deserted. No record exists of the capture of the city.

In the twelfth century, Crusaders built a small fort overlooking the abandoned city, but they were soon driven out. In 1217, a monk named Thelmar visited the site while on a pilgrimage. Then, for nearly 600 years, Petra lay lost to Westerners, until on August 22, 1812, John Lewis Burckhardt walked through the long, narrow cleft in the mountains and made his spectacular discovery.

Left, an early nineteenth-century engraving of El-Deir, whose name means "the monastery." During the Byzantine period, El-Deir was, in fact, used as a monastery. Other buildings were adopted as churches. Until well into this century, the Byzantines were erroneously credited as the builders of the Nabataeans's sophisticated irrigation system.

Church of St. Francis at Assisi

Italy

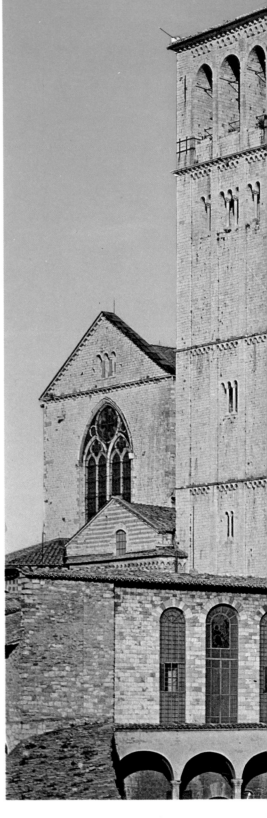

Preceding page, the church of San Francesco, in the town of Assisi, in the Apennines mountains. The church was built as a shrine for Saint Francis, who was born and died in Assisi (1182–1226). Saint Francis, one of the greatest Christian saints, founded the three orders of Franciscans. At the end of his life, he received the stigmata, the wounds of the Crucifixion, which kept him in constant pain. Although he preached and lived the doctrine of poverty, the church which honors him is lavishly decorated with frescoes by such masters as Cimabue and Giotto.

San Francesco (top left) is set on a slope outside the town. The pale stone complex—consisting of a monastery and two churches, one above the other—seems to have become a natural part of the landscape (center left). Bottom left, the row of progressively taller piers that support the buildings.

The lower part of the church is Romanesque, while the upper part displays a marked Gothic influence. Above, the entrances to the lower church, whose doors date from 1300, and the upper church. The outdoor stairway (right) links the two main levels of the church.

Left, the façade of the upper church. With its smooth walls and three distinct horizontal sections, the façade is a typical Italian variation on the Gothic style. (On account of the steep slope, the lower church has no façade in the normal sense of the term.) Above, the rose window and the smaller circular window in the gable which illuminate the space above the vaulted ceiling of the upper church. Right, the upper story of the bell tower. Bartholomew of Pisa, a whimsical bell founder, cast one of the big bells and inscribed upon it his own name and those of Brother Elias, Pope Gregory IX, and Emperor Frederick II. Another of his bells bears the inscription: "I ring in Sunday, I lament for the dead, the lightning I break, I hurry the sluggards, I vanquish the wicked, I disperse the wind."

Top left, the western end of the monastery, whose russet-tinted roofs seem to have taken on the colors of the surrounding countryside. The monastery is built around a series of courtyards and cloisters. San Francesco is now a college for the training of missionaries, in whom the spirit of Saint Francis lives on. Saint Francis founded the Franciscans in 1210 with twelve loyal disciples. By the time of his death, sixteen years later, the order had grown to some 5,000 monks, not including the thousands of laymen in the third order. The poet Dante was a member of this group. The second order of Franciscans is the Poor Clares, an order of nuns founded by Saint Clare.

Center and bottom left, the impressive Chiostro Grande, the central cloister of San Francesco, built during the second half of the fifteenth century by Pope Sixtus IV. There are two arcades on three sides. On the fourth side the upper level gives way before the bulging apse of the double church (right). The horizontal line just above the cloister terrace marks the division between the two churches. On the left, the little door leads to the rooms where the treasures and relics of San Francesco are kept. The former includes rich fifteenth-century tapestries, illuminated missals, ivories, metalwork from the thirteenth century, and a collection of papal bulls of Honorious III. The most prized relics are the gray tunic Saint Francis wore when he died and the felt slippers Saint Clare made for his wounded feet.

Left, the Umbrian countryside, seen from the third story of the bell tower. The mist-filled valley, wrote Henry James, becomes at twilight "a misty counterfeit of the purple sea." Above right, the Romanesque vaults of the lower church, covered in richly hued frescoes. Though many of the frescoes have been ruined by dampness, San Francesco remains "one of the greatest treasure houses of art in all the world."

Below right, a staircase behind the apse of the lower church that leads down to the Neoclassical crypt built in the early nineteenth century. The remains of Saint Francis were placed here in 1230, four years after his death. The tomb of Saint Francis was deliberately hidden by Brother Elias, the leader of the Franciscans after the saint's death. Elias received the remains at the church and then bolted the door on the immense crowd that had come to see the last of the recently canonized and already legendary saint. Aided by a handful of other monks, Elias hid the coffin of their founder in a secret crypt, which was not discovered until the nineteenth century.

Notable among the works by many masters which grace the walls of San Francesco are the splendid frescoes by the Sienese artist Simone Martini. His lively scenes from the life of Saint Martin are characterized by a Gothic spirituality and an elegance of line. Above left, the Emperor Julian knighting Saint Martin. Above right, the saint leaving the service of the emperor. He is offering to confront the enemy armed only with a cross. Above far right, the Vision of Saint Martin. The saint, here depicted as the bishop of Tours, has fallen into such a profound reverie that he is insensitive to the exhortations of the troubled priest at his side.

Below, left to right, Martini's representations of Saint Francis, Saint Louis of Toulouse, Saint Elizabeth, and Saint Clare. Below far right, detail from The Miracle of the Boy.

The upper church (near left), with its sixty-foot vaults, is more pronouncedly Gothic in style than the lower church. The frescoes on the right-hand wall are part of a series of twenty-eight which portray the life and legend of Saint Francis. The frescoes above them are probably by Pietro Cavallini and his pupils.

Above far left, frescoes in the vault of the upper church, thought to be the work of Jacopo Torriti. The medallions in the center of the vaults bear the images of Christ (left) and Saint John (right). The faded colors in the frescoes alongside the window show the effects of age and dampness.

Below far left, the north transept and choir of the upper church. The back walls were once covered with frescoes by Cimabue, Giotto's master. The choir stalls, magnificent examples of intarsia (elaborate, inlaid woodwork), dating from 1501, took Dominico la San Severino ten years to make.

Above, the starry vault of San Francesco.

Above, the choir stalls in the apse of the upper church. The wooden mosaic portraits on their backs depict the friends and followers of Saint Francis.

The stained-glass windows in the upper church date from the early fourteenth century. Those in the apse (left) bear the coat of arms of the Orsini family, great patrons of the church.

Above right, the Apostles John and Andrew, occupying the lower thirds of the lancet windows on the north side of the upper church.

Far right, the intricate rose window. Near right, the windows of the southern transept. The four lancets depict, left to right, the Creation, the Fall of Adam and Eve, and two panels of female saints.

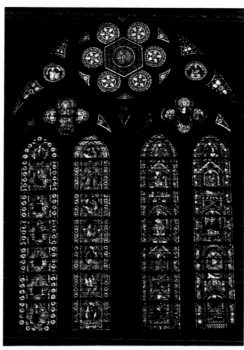

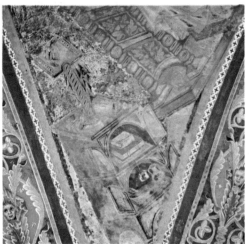

The frescoes of the transept and apse of the upper church are the work of Cimabue. The colors have nearly all faded, yet the artist's mastery of anecdotal detail is still manifest. Below far left, trumpeting angels from Christ the Judge in the southern transept. Above far left, The Crucifixion of Saint Peter from the northern transept. Saint Peter is said to have declared himself unworthy to be crucified in the same manner as Christ: The Romans obliged him in the manner shown. Near left, The Dormition of the Virgin on the southern side of the apse. Above, top to bottom: the bookcase and throne of Saint Mark in the crossing of the upper church; Saint Luke; and a sleepy-looking Saint Matthew, seen in the eastern quadrant of the crossing.

The frescoes in the upper church portraying the life of Saint Francis were once all thought to be by Giotto, but now some are seen as the work of his assistants. Saint Francis (left) preaches to an attentive flock of birds that, in the words of one biographer, "saluted the holy man and bent their heads in attentive expectation." Francis loved animals. One story relates that in his last days he offered profuse apologies to his donkey for having rebuked it.

Above right, part of the fresco Saint Francis Appears at the Council of Aries showing Saint Anthony of Padua. Below left, part of Saint Francis Appears before the Sultan. Giotto later painted a more psychologically interesting version of this scene in Florence. Below center, a detail from Saint Francis in the Chariot of Fire. Below right, detail from The Death of the Count of Celano. Saint Francis, who was one of the count's guests, had advised this nobleman to repent, for his days were numbered. The count did—and fell dead on the table.

Giotto's great series of frescoes about the life of Saint Francis abound in masterful touches. Above, the landscape from Saint Francis Clothing the Poor. *The small town with its few scraggly trees clinging to the cliff is reminiscent of the hillside towns of Giotto's native Tuscany. Below left, an ornamental architectural embellishment in* Saint Francis Receives License to Preach, *remarkable for its naturalism and convincing depiction of receding space. Below right, detail from* The Dream of Saint Francis, *in which Saint Francis saw a gorgeous palace filled with arms and banners bearing the emblem of the cross—a symbol of the spiritual army.*

Right, part of Giotto's Evil Spirits Expulsed from Arezzo. *According to legend, Saint Francis fervently prayed from outside the gates of Arezzo that the city might be rid of its demons. Here, the demons are driven from their dark haunts in chimneys and eaves by his prayers. Giotto's cityscape displays a novel sense of architectural space.*

Following page, San Francesco and Mount Subasio seen from the east—a view which has scarcely changed in 800 years.

Church of St. Francis at Assisi Italy

Some one hundred miles northeast of Rome, the plains of Umbria begin to give way to the rugged foothills of the Apennines. There, in the little town of Assisi, stands one of the great monuments to medieval faith and one of the earliest Gothic churches built in Italy—the church of Saint Francis of Assisi.

San Francesco, as it is known in Italian, was built between 1228 and 1256 as a shrine to the legendary mystic, poet, and spiritual leader whose remains are buried there. The whole complex—an upper and lower church and an adjoining monastery—is architecturally interesting in its own right. But San Francesco is further enhanced by the legend of the saint who

lived in imitation of Christ and died with the stigmata, the wounds of the Crucifixion, upon his body.

The church dedicated to Saint Francis has been called "one of the greatest treasure houses of art in all the world." Its walls are covered with frescoes by Italian masters of the fourteenth century, who introduced the great age of Italian painting, including Giotto himself, the first modern painter. It is somewhat of an irony that the church of Saint Francis should be renowned for its artistic wealth since Francis himself was dedicated to the ideal of poverty, preferring secluded mountain caves to formal houses of God. Even so, the structure of the Franciscan church at Assisi respects Francis's commitment to the democracy of worship: Unlike other Gothic churches, there are no pillars or columns that come between preacher and congregation.

The biographies of most famous persons trace a familiar pattern: the climb from obscurity to worldly success. Far from being ambitious for either fame or wealth, Saint Francis pursued a life of poverty and self-denial. Rebel, mystic, and spiritual leader, Saint Francis has inspired generations of writers, among them

Below left, a nineteenth-century engraving of San Francesco, showing the forecourt of the lower church. Despite Saint Francis's rejection of worldly power, the two great patrons of his church were the rivals of the Emperor Frederick II (bottom), who was the friend and protector of Brother Elias, and Pope Gregory IX (immediately below).

GREGORIVS IX tib.' Signæ Anagni Martij ann.1227. 5.dies 3.Ob.22. Hugolin.'ex Comitinus, creat.'die 20. Sedit an.14.men. Aug. an.1241.V.S.m.i.

Above, a cross section through the transept of the church of Saint Francis, showing the superimposition of the upper over the lower church.

Below, a plan of the lower church. Originally, it was to have been identical to the upper church, but side chapels and the eastern transept were added in the thirteenth and fourteenth centuries.

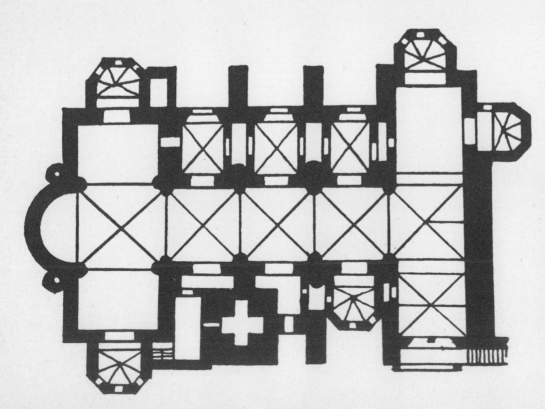

Dante, who placed him above the doctors of the Church and the founders of other monastic orders. Matthew Arnold praised his poetry as the "humble upper waters of a mighty stream; at the beginning of the thirteenth century it is Francis, at the end Dante." The nineteenth-century French historian Renan, who wrote a biography of Saint Francis, called the village of Assisi "the Galilee of Italy;" and in our own time G. K. Chesterton saluted the saint as "a poet whose whole life was a poem."

Believers and skeptics alike admire him for his compassionate identification with the poor, and some even classify Francis as an early socialist. To those of religious conviction, however, Francis was a holy man who heard heavenly voices and who walked in the transforming light of God.

Saint Francis was born around 1181 in a house whose remains are still visible in Assisi. His father, Pietro Bernardone, was a wealthy cloth merchant, who happened to be traveling in France at the time of his son's birth. In her husband's absence, Pica Bernardone christened her baby Giovanni. Legend has it that when Pietro returned he changed the boy's name to Francis in honor of the land where he had first heard the joyful news of his son's birth. It is more likely that Giovanni was renamed Francis some years later, on account of the enthusiasm he displayed for all things French. His mother was French, and the youth took avidly to the French tongue and sang the lays of the troubadours with passion.

Though legends about the young Francis abound, little of his early life is known. According to the pious Thomas of Celano, who was one of his followers and began the first *Life* of the saint within hours of his death, Francis "wasted his life up to his twenty-fifth year, singing without restraint and leading other people his own age into evil. He loved all manner of pleasantry and farces, dressed himself up in women's garments, threw away money with both hands. . . . So he went on till the day when the hand of the Lord weighed down upon and transformed him."

Contemporary biographers take a less severe view of his early life. "One cannot

Right, the interior of the eastern transept of the lower church, looking into a fourteenth-century chapel. The heavy, decorated groin vaults are graceful despite the limited height; in comparison, the thirteenth-century apse of the lower church (below right) has a more cryptlike quality as compared to the lighter, more vertical Gothic lines of the upper church.

Left, an engraving of the rose window over the southern entrance of the lower church. The delicately carved stone tracery is typical of such Italian windows of the thirteenth century.

imagine him," one scholar writes, "as corrupted or corruptor, and if there were some failings and weaknesses in his life, there were assuredly no villainies." Francis was probably no more than a carefree, high-spirited youth, who traveled with his father from fair to fair and dreamt of becoming a soldier.

Francis grew up in an atmosphere of war. For thirty years before his birth, Assisi had been fighting for its independence, first against the Holy Roman Empire and then against its own feudal aristocracy, who had sided with the German princes in the earlier struggle. After finally achieving its independence, Assisi was plunged into a war against its predatory neighbor, Perugia, in a struggle which lasted several more years (1201–1209). According to Pope Innocent III, "Not only had war, with its orgies and anarchy, become a habit and a necessity in Assisi, but it was the preferred occupation, the favorite passion and, in fact, the raison d'être of this town where the word peace had no meaning."

In 1202, Francis proudly became a soldier of his native city. He fought with distinction against Perugia and was taken prisoner at the battle of Ponte San Giovanni on the Tiber. He was held captive for nearly a year and on his release fell gravely ill. From that time on he suffered severe recurrent attacks of tuberculosis, which may have ultimately caused his death.

While in prison, Francis is said to have remarked, "One day I'll be the idol of the whole world." Doubtless it was military glory he aspired to, for within months of regaining his health, he enlisted in yet another, still larger, war between the papacy and the Holy Roman Empire. He set off with his squire behind him, but on the very first night a voice commanded him in his sleep to return home. His conversion had begun.

Shortly after returning to Assisi he had a second mysterious visitation. One day, stopping to pray at a disused chapel near Assisi called San Damiano, Francis was astonished to hear a voice command him from the altar crucifix, "Go and repair my house which, as thou seest, is wholly fallen into ruin." Francis took this message literally. He used—more candid biographers say "stole"—his father's money to rebuild the crumbling San Damiano and other abandoned chapels, including San Maria della Portiuncula which, according to Saint Bonaventure, became the place that Francis loved most in the world. It still stands very close to San Francesco.

Francis's father took him to court over the "borrowed" funds. Francis defended himself by saying that he was carrying out the will of his Heavenly Father. In a dramatic gesture, he renounced his earthly father, taking off and returning the rich clothes his father had given him. A shock went through the bishop's court when Francis cast off the last of his garments to reveal a penitent's hair shirt.

Francis continued to rebuild churches for a year or two, though at times he had to beg for money and even for stones. But while attending mass at the Portiuncula chapel, he suddenly realized that he had misunderstood his first summons. As the priest read the admonition of Jesus to "heal the sick, cleanse the lepers, freely ye receive, freely give...," Francis understood his true calling. To do the work of God, he must help the poor; he must be a spiritual builder rather than a literal builder of churches.

Above right, the apse of the upper church, flooded with light from its tall Gothic windows.

Above left and left, nineteenth-century pen drawings by Lorenzo Carpinelli and Giovanni Battista Mariani looking east and west from the transept of the upper church. The rose window above the entrance is clearly visible (above left).

Earlier, Francis had symbolically shed his father's clothes. Now he adopted a dun-colored monk's tunic with a simple rope around the middle, which would become the humble uniform of the order he was to found.

From that time on Francis spent his life preaching. He traveled through Italy and beyond—to Spain, to the wilds of Slavonia, even to Syria. His call for voluntary poverty stirred the consciences of young men all over Europe. His order grew rapidly. By the time he died, there were some 5,000 Franciscan monks. They became known as the Poor Ones and Francis himself was called Il Poverello, the "little poor man."

Certain episodes stand out in Francis's life, among them his encounter with the daughter of an influential count in Assisi. Accustomed to the privileges of an aristocratic life, she shocked her parents when she left her family to practice the teachings of Saint Francis. After a year-long novitiate, she entered the convent of San Damiano, where she vowed herself to chastity and the "privilege of poverty." The maiden was the future Saint Clare, who founded the Poor Clares, the second order of Franciscans.

Francis also undertook a quixotic mission to end the Crusades, in the belief that it was better not to kill Moslems but to convert them. He traveled to Damietta in Syria, where he was captured and taken before the sultan. Francis asked that a fire be kindled and offered to pass through it if the Moslem spiritual leaders would do the same, as a test of their respective faiths. The sultan declined the offer but set Francis free, in tribute to his zeal. Giotto later painted a fresco of this now-famous scene in which the eyes of the saint express a terrible melancholy: His mission of peace had failed.

Above right, a plan of the upper church, which is brighter, simpler, and less warrenlike than the lower church.

Right, an engraving of the upper church. The portal is quintessentially Gothic, but the horizontally divided façade above it is more characteristic of Italian architecture in general than of a particular architectural style.

The last years of Francis's life were beset with suffering, both mental and physical. His order was almost split over the rule of poverty, and after 1220, his health broke. Francis had patterned his life after Christ, and in August 1224, he became the first person in history to suffer the stigmata—the wounds suffered by Christ during his Crucifixion.

Worn down by the incessant factional wrangles in his order, Francis had gone into seclusion on Monte La Verna, a mountain north of Assisi, near the source of the Arno. He climbed the 4,000 feet to the summit and remained there alone for over a month, praying to God that he might suffer the awful glory of Christ's Passion. On September 13, his prayers were answered. Just before dawn he saw an angel in the golden air. As it drew near, Francis saw that its wings were nailed to a cross. In the next instant he felt an excruciating pain, and when he looked down, he saw the marks of nails in his palms, a small wound gleaming red in his left side, and holes in his feet. When he died two years later, his body still bore the scars of these wounds.

Despite his suffering, Francis's poetry is full of joy. The *Canticle of the Sun*, written

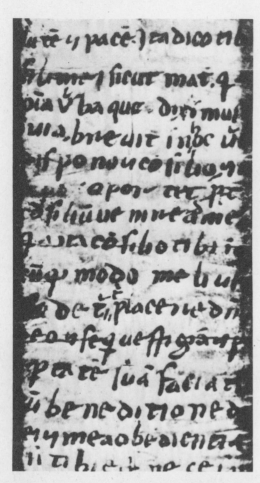

Right, a print of Saint Francis dictating the rules of his order. The seals under the book bear the names of the popes who approved and sometimes modified the rules of the order.

just before he died, speaks of his joy in all created things, in Brother Sun and Sister Moon and Mother Earth; joy at the daily miracle of existence; joy, even, at the last, in Sister Death.

Francis would have probably disapproved of the magnificent church built in his honor. Yet in one way at least, the church of San Francesco is a fulfillment of his joyful spirit. San Francesco was built in a display of extraordinary generosity. Soon after Pope Gregory IX laid the cornerstone in 1228, contributions for the building of a church poured in from all over Europe, and even from Jerusalem. The peasants of the area had no money but gave generously of their labor. Work progressed so rapidly that, in May 1230, barely four years after the saint's death, the lower church was ready to receive his

remains.

San Francesco lies just outside the town of Assisi, on the northwest end of a ridge known as Monte Subasio. The faded buff colors of the church blend with the soft tones of the surrounding countryside, in harmony with its setting. San Francesco consists of two churches built one above the other on the hillside. Building was begun with the church at the top of the hill. Later additions to the monastery below the two churches were made progressively down the slope.

The churches are laid out in more or less identical patterns and are linked by an outdoor stairway. The major difference between them is that the forecourt of the upper church lies to the east, while that of the lower church faces the south. The churches are unusual in that they are oriented backward: The altars necessarily

lie to the west rather than the east so that the congregation can enter from ground level at the opposite end.

The church itself was consecrated in 1253, but the construction of the other monastic buildings—refectories, chapter houses, and cloisters—continued throughout the thirteenth and fourteenth centuries. The cloister behind the double church was not completed until 1476, and one building was added as late as the eighteenth century.

No one is sure who the architect of San Francesco was, though some think it was a certain James of Germany or the masters Comacini. The driving spirit behind the construction, however, was the first vicar-general of the Franciscan order, the indefatigable Brother Elias.

Elias was dissatisfied with the rule of poverty. He wanted the order to become a power in the world—to own churches and monasteries of its own rather than to give its property to the poor. While Francis had gone barefoot, Elias moved about Italy with an entourage, like a bishop. Both in their way were typical medieval men: Francis the extreme, "primitive" Christian and Elias the ecclesiastical politician.

Pope Gregory IX also had a hand in getting the church built. When the pontiff made known his wish to build a church in honor of Saint Francis, a generous citizen of Assisi donated the present site. At that time, the hill was called the Collis Inferni, for criminals had once been executed there. Gregory changed the name to Collis Paradisi, the Hill of Paradise, in tribute to the extraordinary view from San Francesco at twilight. In the words of Henry James, it "embraces the whole wide reach of Umbria, which becomes as twilight deepens a purple counterfeit of the misty sea."

Most striking about San Francesco's interior is its openness, an immense awe-inspiring space beneath soaring vaults. This democratic structure mirrors a central tenet of Francis's philosophy: that religious life should not be separate from the common life. Even the immensity of the church is not intimidating. The beautiful lancet windows behind the altar filter in a constant stream of light, making this a

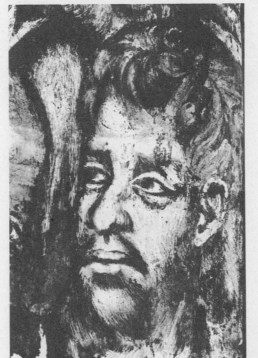

Left, detail from Cimabue's Crucifixion *scene in the southern transept of the upper church. This fascinating face is believed to be that of Cimabue. Immediately below, an engraving by Seroux d'Agincourt (1826), showing Cimabue's fresco of* The Assumption of the Virgin *in the apse.*

Below, reconstructions of the works of Cimabue in San Francesco. Left to right, three versions of The Fall of Simon Magnus—*the first by Seroux d'Agincourt, the second a drawing by Jacopo Grimaldi (1560–1623), and the third a water color by Johann Ramboux (1790–1866);* The Decapitation of Saint Paul *by Grimaldi; and* The Crucifixion of Saint Peter, *a water color by Ramboux.*

Above, the most beautiful stained-glass windows at San Francesco, from Saint Martin's chapel in the lower church. They may have been designed by Simone Martini, who painted the frescoes in the chapel.

Above right, a nineteenth-century portrait of Giotto. Right, a nineteenth-century engraving of the artist Cimabue admiring the artistic precocity of a shepherd boy drawing with a piece of charcoal. The boy was Giotto. It may have been Cimabue who persuaded the twenty-nine-year-old Giotto to work on the walls of San Francesco. Just which frescoes were executed by Giotto and which were done by his students remains uncertain to this day.

church in which to praise God, not fear Him.

Henry James was deeply moved by the lower church. "You seem to push into the very heart of Catholicism... The tone of the place is a triumph of mystery, the richest harmony of lurking shadows and dusty corners, all relieved by scattered images and scintillations." The side chapels of the lower church are covered with dark, barely visible frescoes. James calls attention to a primitive fresco of the Crucifixion by Pietro Cavallini, one of Giotto's pupils: "You will nowhere see anything more direfully lugubrious. The most poignant touch is the tragic grimaces of the little angelic heads that fall like hailstones through the dark air behind the Cross."

Every inch of wall and vaulting at San Francesco is covered with frescoes by the early masters of Italian art—Pisano, Simone Martini, and Cimabue. There are also several frescoes by Giotto, who was a member of the Tertiary order, or lay ver-

sion, of the Franciscans. Among the works attributed to him are the series of frescoes in the lower church known as *The Legend of Saint Francis*. Though many think that these lesser works were executed by one of Giotto's pupils, it is generally agreed that the more accomplished scenes from the Isaac cycle in the upper story of the church were the work of the master himself.

Saint Francis died on October 3, 1226. Knowing that his end was near, he was carried to the Portiuncula, the tiny chapel that had been the first meeting place of the order. Here, stretched on the earth, he sang the last verse of his *Canticle of the Sun,* which he had composed for the occasion, and died in peace.

Through the centuries, his spirit has lived on in the conviction of his followers. During World War II, for example, Father Rufino Nicacci turned San Francesco into a hiding place for Jewish refugees. He dressed them as monks, forged their identity papers, and sequestered them in the

monastery under the eyes of the occupying Germans. In return, one of the refugees saved San Francesco. The Germans were seriously considering bombing the church to slow up the Allied advance, but this resourceful refugee, disguised as a monk, used his command of German to negotiate an "open cities" agreement with them. San Francesco was spared.

The Germans would have razed San Francesco had they known it was harboring Jews. Father Nicacci thus risked the destruction of this magnificent church to save the lives of those of another faith—a testimony to the spirit of brotherhood preached by Saint Francis centuries before at Assisi.

Palatine Chapel
at Aachen

West Germany

Preceding page, the finest extant monument of the Carolingian dynasty—the Palatine Chapel of Charlemagne in Aachen, West Germany. In A.D. 800, Charlemagne made Aachen the capital of his empire, which stretched from the North Sea to the Mediterranean. Five years later, Pope Leo III dedicated the emperor's palace chapel. The remaining original sections of the chapel include the structure of the octagonal chapel (in the center, above) and the lower parts of the west-work (right).

The exterior of the chapel was altered significantly between 1353 and 1413 with the addition of a Gothic choir and many flanking chapels (on the left above). The Gothic verticality of the choir's apse (left) stands in sharp contrast to the massive forms of the Carolingian octagon.

The lower, Carolingian section of the westwork (right) contains the entrance to the chapel—framed by a large masonry arch—and two stairways leading up to the tribune where Charlemagne sat during services. At one time, the westwork housed a small reliquary chapel in which Charlemagne safeguarded a cape once worn by Saint Martin—from which, it is said, the word "chapel" originated. The Gothic addition above the arch holds a small chapel crowned by a nineteenth-century spire.

The bronze doors of the westwork (top), emblazoned with lion heads (immediately above), were cast at Charlemagne's own foundry in 804.

The heart of Charlemagne's palace chapel—now to be seen only through the eyes of its fourteenth-century restorers—is the three-tiered octagon with its crowning mosaic dome (above center). The cross-vaulted ground floor and ambulatory (top left) were used by Charlemagne's subjects; the upper gallery (center left), spanned by massive striped arches, was set aside for the emperor himself and his court. This private gallery was originally connected by an enclosed passageway to the palace, permitting Charlemagne and his entourage to attend services without passing through the ground floor below. The emperor's simple white marble throne (bottom left) directly faces the altar to the east across the octagon. Tall arcade arches (far right, above and below), subdivided by the screen of Corinthian columns, symbolically direct worshipers' thoughts toward heaven. The bronze chandelier (near right), with sixteen turrets and forty-eight lamps, was a gift of Frederick Barbarossa in 1168. It hangs at the center of the dome above the traditionally ascribed site of Charlemagne's tomb.

The chapel's mosaic dome (right, viewed through Frederick Barbarossa's chandelier) is the work of the Italian Antonio Salviati. In 1881, he attempted to reproduce the original Carolingian mosaic from a seventeenth-century drawing. The choir (above) built between 1353 and 1413, echoes St. Chapelle, the high-Gothic royal chapel in Paris. The delicate Gothic construction of the choir complements the weightier, and more heavily decorated, Carolingian octagon. Below, the upper gallery of the Chapel of St. Nicholas, which probably once served as an entrance to a covered colonnade connecting the church and the palace.

The cathedral's treasury, the richest in Germany, contains illuminated manuscripts, ivories, gold work, and paintings. Among the valuable artifacts in the chapel are a golden altar front (top left) which dates from the time of Emperor Otto III (ca. 1000); a sixteenth-century panel depicting Mary as the "new Eve" (top right); a reliquary made in 1215 to house Charlemagne's skull (center left); and the reliquary of Saint Mary finished in 1238 (immediately above). Two late-Roman bronzes—a pine cone (far left) and a she-wolf (near left)—stand on opposite sides of the church's vestibule. Carolingian bronze railings are set within the gallery arcade (near right). A late-Gothic corridor (above right) leads to the treasury museum (far right).

Following page, the original eighth-century Carolingian wall of the Palatine Chapel of Charlemagne.

Palatine Chapel at Aachen West Germany

About two-thirds of the German city of Aachen was destroyed during World War II bombing raids. Fortunately, however, the city's greatest historic treasure—the Palatine Chapel of Charlemagne—was spared. Founded by Charlemagne, king of the Franks and emperor of the West, the medieval group of chapel buildings still looms above the streets of the old town. The splendid octagonal chapel and soaring late-Gothic choir are a quiet reminder of past glory, of the days when Aachen, or Aix-la-Chapelle, as it is known in French, was the focus of the Carolingian dynasty. From here Charlemagne ruled his empire, exerting political and cultural dominion over the medieval Western world.

The Palatine Chapel, which still houses Charlemagne's remains, is the greatest surviving monument of the Carolingian era. Built from 789 to 794 A.D.. the chapel is an outward symbol of the union of political and ecclesiastical power achieved by its sovereign. In its construction, Charlemagne sought to emulate the architectural monuments of his Eastern predecessors, the emperors Constantine and Justinian, and thereby reinforce his position as a comparable potentate of the West.

From 500 to 751, the Merovingian dynasty of Frankish kings ruled over a sizable portion of northern Europe. From early in the seventh century, however, Charlemagne's forebears, beginning with Pepin of Landen, had been the de facto rulers of the Frankish kingdom of Austrasia—a region covering eastern France, western Germany, and parts of Belgium and the Netherlands. Charlemagne's father, Pepin the Short, was the first of the line to actually usurp the crown. In response to an appeal by Pope Stephen II, whose holy city of Rome was being threatened by its Lombard neighbors, Pepin led two military campaigns into Italy finally defeating the Lombards in 756. In return, Pepin was annointed king by the pope. This papal blessing on the Carolingian kingdom marked the beginning of a crucial political alliance between the pope and the Franks.

Charlemagne, or Charles the Great, was the eldest son of Pepin. Born in 742, he inherited the willfulness and religious conviction of his father. Tall and strong, he was well suited for the rigors of war and throughout his youth accompanied his father on military expeditions. Although he never learned to read, he was of quick intelligence, mastering Latin and Greek and studying rhetoric, dialectics, and astronomy. But Charlemagne's greatest strength was his sense of mission. It is largely because of his religious fervor, combined with a determination to rule, that he has gone down in history as an exemplar of a Christian king and emperor.

Upon the death of his father in 768 and his brother Carloman in 771, Charlemagne assumed complete control. When the Lombard King Desiderius invaded papal territories in 772, Charlemagne and his troops quickly responded to a summons from Pope Adrian. After a year-long campaign, the Lombard kingdom fell, making Charlemagne king of the Lombards as well as the Franks. Spurred on by victory, he renewed his attacks on Saxony, which he ultimately conquered.

Within a decade, Charlemagne's military successes made him the most powerful ruler in Europe. He strove to unify his empire by demanding its common allegiance to the Christian faith. He continued Pepin's policy of ecclesiastical reform and strenuously opposed the Eastern doctrine of iconoclasm. When Pope Leo III was charged with misconduct by personal enemies in 800, he cleared himself under

The jeweled, gold reliquary bust (near right) was made in 1215 to hold Charlemagne's skull.

Far right, a "bird's-eye view" of medieval Aachen. The imperial complex at the center is encircled by both the original town wall and a second wall, which had to be built as the town prospered and expanded.

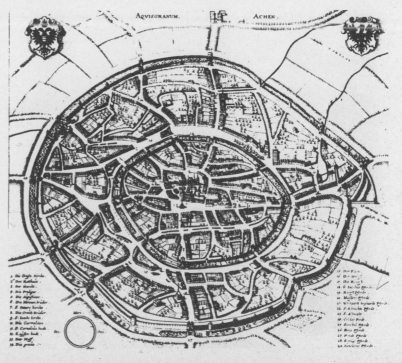

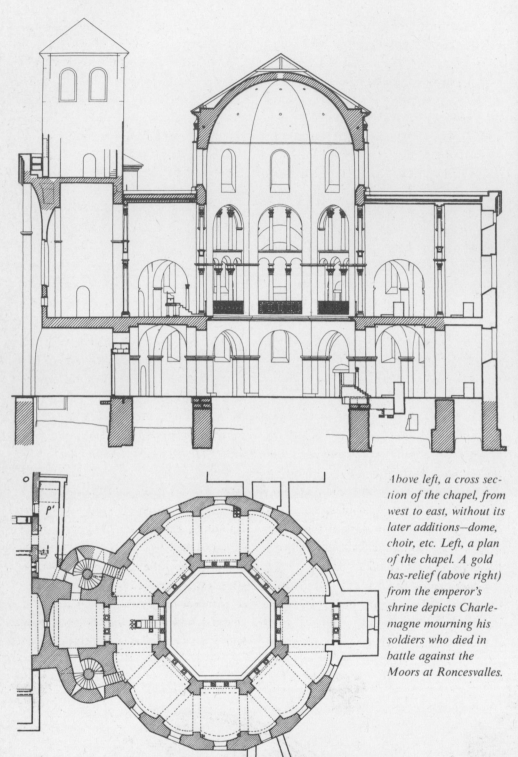

Above left, a cross section of the chapel, from west to east, without its later additions—dome, choir, etc. Left, a plan of the chapel. A gold bas-relief (above right) from the emperor's shrine depicts Charlemagne mourning his soldiers who died in battle against the Moors at Roncesvalles.

solemn oath in a court presided over by Charlemagne. Then, during Christmas mass in St. Peter's two days later, the Pope crowned Charlemagne emperor of the West—an act which confirmed the split between Byzantium and Rome.

From all sides, Charlemagne was proclaimed the new David, the new Constantine. As both rulers had done before him, Charlemagne founded an impressive imperial city from which to rule his empire. Aachen, his capital, was located in the old

kingdom of Austrasia, the original home of the Carolingians. In addition to its strategic proximity to troublesome Saxony, Aachen offered the pleasures of health-giving springs—famous since Roman times—and hunting grounds.

Using the spoils of his victories, Charlemagne commissioned a royal residence and chapel that were to rival those of Rome and Byzantium. Aachen's imperial buildings, therefore, were intended to be a deliberate evocation of the architectural

forms of the older empires and the implicit authority which they represented. In short, Charlemagne's architect, Odo of Metz, was to make Aachen and the palace into a "second Rome."

Odo built the palace around the mineral springs, including a thermal swimming pool which could hold over one hundred men. At the opposite end of the 650-foot-long courtyard stood the Palatine Chapel, which is largely inspired by the sixth-century Byzantine church of San Vitale in Ravenna in northern Italy. Built by Justinian, San Vitale is in its turn based on an imperial prototype—that of Hagia Sophia. (Ravenna itself had once been another "new Rome.") Charlemagne must have hoped that Odo's own interpretation of San Vitale would give the new court an appearance similar to the court at Constantinople, which to Western eyes represented the acme of majesty.

Both laborers and materials for the chapel came from foreign lands—Italy, England, Ireland, and perhaps the East. Charlemagne even obtained license from Pope Adrian to import marble from antique buildings in Italy for the church's columns and floors. He also required his vassals to send artisans to Aachen and imposed such rigorous schedules that the

chapel was completed in five years.

The chapel is a huge octagon, 50 feet in diameter and 110 in height, that rises through four stories to a mosaicked octagonal dome. The chapel is encircled by a ground-floor ambulatory corridor and a tall upper-level gallery, both separated from the main space by arcades and both, like the central dome, skillfully vaulted—an indication of the high degree of technical competence of these early medieval masons. The gallery is covered by high barrel vaults, some sloping steeply toward the exterior, between which are lower, smaller, triangular vaults. On the ground-floor ambulatory, cross vaults alternate with triangular vaults of the same height. Both vaulting arrangements answered the need to link the octagonal, central space with the sixteen-sided exterior wall surrounding the ambulatory and gallery.

The clerestory above the gallery arcade is encrusted with golden mosaics and pierced by large windows. Contrast with the dark voids of the arcades below draws the eye upward, toward the dome of heaven. This three-tiered construction symbolizes, both in design and function, the relationship of the emperor and the people to God. Charlemagne's white marble throne is located in the second-story

Above left, a miniature of 1180 representing Frederick Barbarossa. Above right, Charlemagne (at left) with a model of the cathedral in Bremen, West Germany. Below, an eleventh-century illustration of Charlemagne's tomb at Aachen.

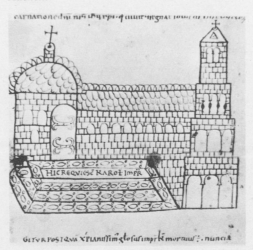

gallery, or tribune. There, between the common people and heaven but on the same elevated level as the main altar, Charlemagne could attend the services. The throne, positioned above the church's main portal, faces the altar of Christ the Savior directly opposite on the east side of the gallery. The gallery, whose arcade is double the height of that below, is further separated from the central space by a two-storied screen of rare and beautiful antique porphyry columns from Rome,

Ravenna, and Trier supplemented by a bronze railing of extreme delicacy.

The chapel was entered through an imposing, fortresslike western façade, or westwork, which symbolized Charlemagne's role as defender of the Church. As in many other churches, this distinctively Carolingian feature contained an upper-level chapel from which the emperor could look down toward the altar at the east end. Even in his absence it represented the symbiotic relationship between church and state and served as an emblematic surrogate for the emperor himself—Charlemagne's power to some extent being based on his personal presence throughout the empire.

The westwork at Aachen consists of two large stair towers, one on either side of the arched entrance, that give access to the emperor's tribune inside. Previously, it had been preceded by a colonnaded atrium with galleries on two levels on the north and south sides and a monumental entranceway at its western front. The emperor could make appearances from these galleries, addressing the people—as many as 7,000—in the courtyard below. There were also twin basilican churches to the north and south sides of the main chapel.

As with the elaborate westwork, the

geometric solidity of Aachen differs markedly from the more complex spatial unity of its prototype in Ravenna. Unlike Aachen, the encircling upper gallery in the Greek Orthodox church of San Vitale (probably reserved for women) held no imperial tribune and does not continue around the eastern end—where the altar is located on the ground floor.

But in the internal arrangements and decoration of the two churches, the honor due to God is inextricably linked to that due his earthly representatives. Thus, both the original mosaics of the apse of San Vitale and the dome of Aachen symbolize the divine authority of the rulers. The mosaic on Aachen's dome showed the twenty-four elders of the Apocalypse laying down their crowns before Christ, while at San Vitale, Justinian and his Empress Theodora are all but identified as Christ and Mary. The implicit message in both is the same: The rule of kings and emperors is but an earthly reflection of the divine government of the universe.

The Carolingian empire existed intact for only one generation after Charlemagne, but Aachen remained for centuries the emperor's chapel. In 972, the Holy Roman Emperor Otto the Great designated Aachen "the coronation city." From the death of Louis II in 840 to the time of Emperor Ferdinand in 1558, thirty-six kings and ten queens were crowned within its walls. During these years several important alterations were made. A fire in 1224 destroyed the imperial palace and a large part of the town. An immense Gothic choir was built during the years 1353 to 1413 in place of the apse of Charlemagne's time. Its thirteen windows, eighty-four feet high, run together in almost uninterrupted walls of luminescent color. The exterior of Odo's dome also underwent changes, receiving first some thirteenth-century triangular gables and then a fluted sixteenth-century dome and cupola.

In 1730, the interior walls were overlaid with a clutter of Baroque stucco relief putti, medallions, and flowers. In the late nineteenth century these were replaced with new marble veneers and the unremarkable mosaics of the Italian Antonio Salviati, who attempted to reproduce the originals as shown in a seventeenth-century drawing. Almost all the surfaces in the interior date from this restoration.

The antique columns also did not go unnoticed. Napoleon had them removed to Paris, but in 1843, all but seven were re-erected—the remainder being replaced by copies. Although some of Aachen's ecclesiastical treasures have been lost to wars and plunderers, many priceless objects survive. Hanging above the white floor inscribed *Carlo Magno,* which marks the supposed site of Charlemagne's tomb, is an immense bronze chandelier. More than thirteen feet in diameter, it was commissioned by Frederick Barbarossa and hand wrought by the master Wilbert of Aachen. Its eight large and eight small turrets and forty-eight candles symbolize the heavenly Jerusalem. The golden altar front and ornate pulpit of gold and Egyptian ivory both date from the eleventh century. In the gallery is a marble Roman sarcophagus, upon which is a bas-relief of the rape of Proserpina. It is said to have held the remains of Charlemagne before they were placed in the golden ark where they rest today. The treasury itself contains such precious artifacts as Charlemagne's hunting horn, Roman cameos, reliquaries, crowns, and statues.

Above all, the Palatine Chapel is a monument to the genius of one man, who breathed life and spirit into an empire whose political and civic achievements were not to be surpassed for centuries. Appropriately, the vision of Charlemagne is preserved for all time beneath the chapel vaults: *Renovatum est imperium in nomine Christi* ("The empire is renewed in the name of Christ").

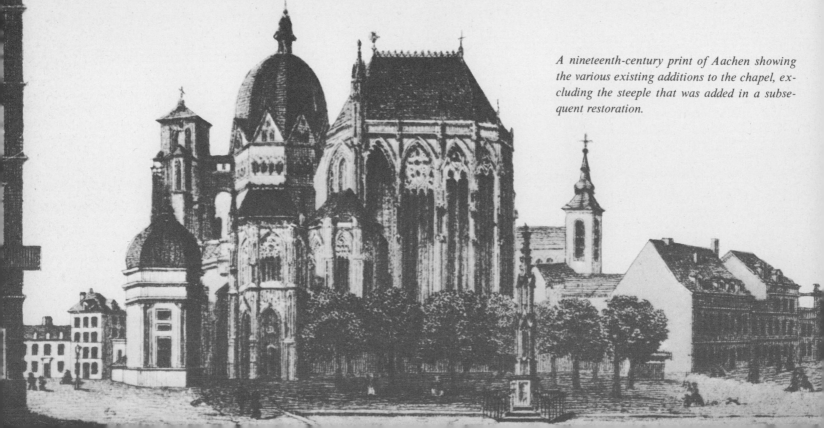

A nineteenth-century print of Aachen showing the various existing additions to the chapel, excluding the steeple that was added in a subsequent restoration.

Cathedral at Monreale

Sicily

Preceding page, the monastery and cathedral at Monreale, near Palermo in Sicily. Monreale was one of the favorite hunting resorts of the Norman kings who governed the island of Sicily in the twelfth century. The cathedral (to the right), founded by William II in 1174, is important both for its unusual blend of diverse architectural styles—Norman, Italian, and Saracen—and its rich Byzantine mosaics. In the foreground stands the archbishop's palace. To the left of the cloister are the ruins of a medieval Benedictine monastery, and in the background stands a more recent seminary.

Situated at the heart of the medieval monastery, the cloister (this page) lends itself to prayer and meditation. The immense square garden, with sides 170 feet long, is a reminder of the perfection of God's creation. Perhaps the most beautiful Romanesque monument in Sicily, the cloister is famous for its ideal proportions, its elegantly decorative paired columns, and the originality of its sculpted capitals. The 228 coupled columns, all of white marble, are enlivened with patterned mosaic inlays in straight, spiral, or zigzag patterns; others are covered with reliefs and tiny grotesques.

Right, the Moorish fountain, which stands in the southwest corner of the cloister. The shaft is surmounted by a cluster of small lion heads whose mouths spout jets of water. The pointed arches of the arcade are also distinctly Arabic.

Above, the south side of the cathedral seen from the cloister. The massive proportions and austere grandeur are characteristically Romanesque. Small windows filter a somber light into the interior. The dome near the tower is that of the Chapel of St. Catherine, which was added at the end of the sixteenth century.

Left, the façade of the cathedral, with its two military-looking Norman towers. The left one was never completed. The entrance portico between the towers is an eighteenth-century addition. The original cathedral façade is ornamented with interlacing arches in an Arabic style—a motif which is also seen on the exterior of the apse. The eclectic mixture of architectural traditions is typical of the Norman reign in Sicily.

Right, the deservedly famous exterior of the cathedral's three apses, ornamented with a richer version of the motif on the façade. The slender, purely ornamental columns are united by interlaced, nonfunctional arches of white limestone and black volcanic lava, between which are similarly mosaicked bands and circles.

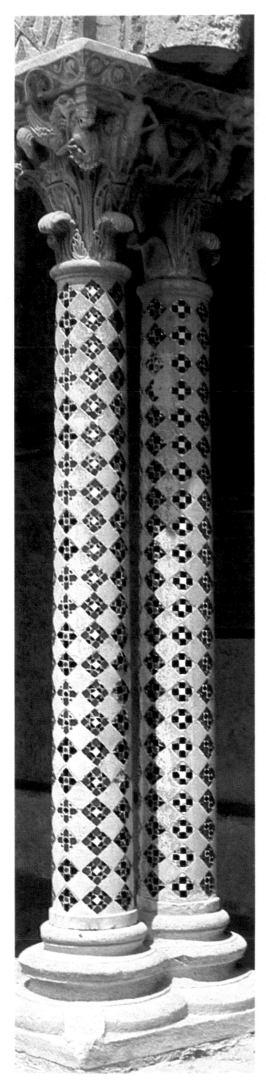

Above and right, the eastern wing of the cloister. The capitals of the cloister columns abound with Biblical, historical, and mythological subjects: saints and pagan gods, nymphs and genii, hunting scenes, birds, sirens, and fantastic monsters. Each scene is set picturesquely against exuberant floral backgrounds.

Top near left, William II of Sicily offering the Virgin a model of the cathedral, which is held by an angel.

Center near left and far left, two youths flanking drinking birds, possibly peacocks. The flesh of the peacock was held to be incorruptible; thus the scene may represent Christians achieving immortality by partaking of the chalice.

Bottom near left, an old man and a young man clinging to vine tendrils that may possibly represent the True Vine on which the Christian is grafted through participation in Christ.

Left, the sanctuary and apse, from which the great Christ Pantocrator (whose upraised hand alone measures over six feet) dominates the church. Above, the painted and gilded wooden roof of the crossing tower. The octagonal coffering reflects a strong Arabic influence. The mosaics on the walls depict the life of Christ.

Below, details of the Byzantine mosaics. Covering 70,400 square feet of the interior, they illustrate the entire story of Christianity, from the Creation to the life and Passion of Christ and the teachings of his disciples. Monreale's mosaic cycle is one of the most magnificent and extensive examples of this Byzantine art form in existence. Below left, Adam and Eve with the Serpent; center, Adam laboring after his expulsion from Paradise; and right, the drunkenness of Noah.

Following page, view of the cathedral apse as it appears from one of Monreale's narrow city streets in a residential area.

Cathedral at Monreale Sicily

According to tradition, in the year 1016 a band of Norman pilgrims returning to France from Jerusalem stopped to visit the shrine of Saint Michael at Monte Gargano in Italy. There the Lombard nobleman, Melus of Bari, persuaded them to join forces with him against the Byzantines. The military prowess of the Normans, coupled with a stature that must have appeared gigantic to the people of the south, assured their eventual success. Subsequently, other Norman mercenaries came to fight in southern Italy and Sicily, against both Byzantium and the Saracens. Their victories were soon rewarded with fiefdoms in the newly conquered lands.

After only fifty or sixty years, the newcomers had consolidated their political and military power over the many resident cultures, even to the point of establishing a monarchy. In 1059, the Normans wisely pledged their allegiance to the pope, more or less legitimizing their conquests. In 1060, these now-undisputed lords of the formerly Byzantine lands of southern Italy were ready to turn toward Moslem Sicily. And by 1071, they had vanquished the Arabs in Sicily as well.

For 200 years, from the mid-ninth century onward, Sicily had been a Saracen province, although the population of the island also included Greeks, Italians, and Jews. Just as they had done in France, and later in England, the Normans proved to be moderate, conciliatory, and able administrators, skillfully assimilating the diverse traditions in Sicily. Although the conquest of Sicily had been violent, there was surprisingly little friction between the northerners and their new subjects. A

Norman charter insured that the members of each community—Norman, Greek, Arab, Lombard, Jew—would be judged according to their own codes of law. The Normans also permitted freedom of religion, even as the rest of Europe was becoming increasingly intolerant.

The kings themselves spoke Norman French, but they issued decrees in Latin, Arabic, and Greek. They appointed Norman barons, Arab admirals and administrators, Moslem or Lombard bankers, French, Lombard, or English bishops, and Greek bureaucrats—exploiting the strengths and talents of their different subjects.

Court ceremonies and protocol derived from Byzantine models. The kings themselves adapted local ways. For public cer-

emonies they wore robes that were embroidered with lines from the Koran and with Greek patterns. Members of the imperial court also frequented harems. In fact, one of the kings, Roger II, was reputed to have kept a harem for his own use. However, the women were said to have withdrawn into penitential seclusion when Saladin conquered Jerusalem in 1187.

The Normans were exceedingly pious Christians. Their faith combined with their abilities on the battlefield made them the main military support of the papacy against its many secular challenges. Indeed, Norman-occupied Sicily was often

Left, Robert Guiscard (1015–1085), William II's ancestor and the founder of Norman power in southern Italy. Together with his brothers, he conquered and united the regions of Apulia, Calabria, and Sicily, creating one of the most powerful states in the Mediterranean. In his development from the leader of a small group of mercenaries to conqueror, Robert proved himself a shrewd and perceptive political figure. He was also an extremely religious man who initiated the tradition of endowing cathedrals and abbeys to give thanks to God as well as to strengthen the Norman influence in his newly conquered territories.

Below, monks strolling in the monastery cloister at Monreale. The 228 pairs of columns supporting the arcade of the covered passageway are decorated with a seemingly unending variety of motifs.

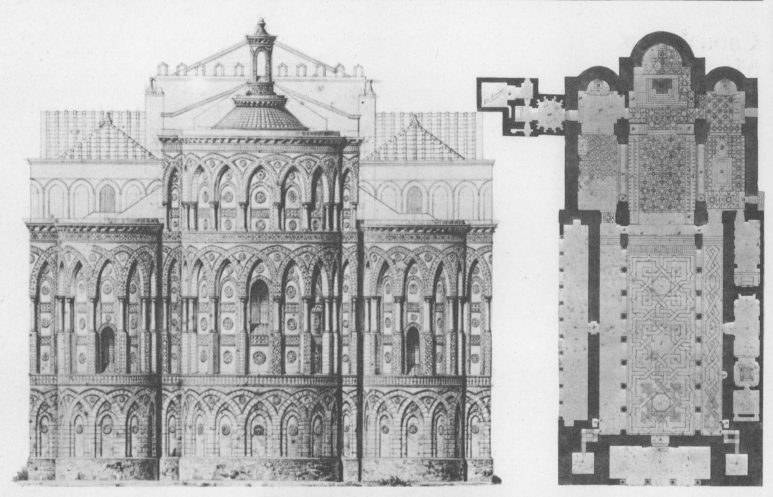

described as being surrounded "on three sides by salt water (the sea) and on the fourth by holy water (the papal state)." The Normans often gave thanks to God for victory in battle by endowing new churches or monasteries. It was this blend of religious sentiments and political concerns that inspired the cathedral at Monreale, one of the finest surviving examples of the architecture that emerged during the two centuries of Norman rule in Sicily.

According to legend, the Norman King William II—known as William the Good to distinguish him from his less scrupulous father—built Monreale at the urging of the Virgin Mary. During a hunt on the royal grounds at Monreale, about five miles south of Palermo, the king purportedly fell asleep under a huge carob tree. The Virgin appeared to him in a dream and commanded him to build a church. She promised him that under the carob tree he would find a treasure of gold, silver, and precious stones that he should use to build a magnificent monument.

Top right, a plan of the cathedral showing, from bottom to top: the entrance porch flanked by the two towers, the nave with its two side aisles, and the almost square transept and sanctuary terminated by the three apses. Top left, a drawing of the highly ornamented exterior of the triple apse. Above, a typical medieval manuscript illumination of a Norman king displaying a cathedral he has built as an offering to God.

Skeptics claim that this story was invented only to justify the huge sums of money William lavished on the cathedral. And, in fact, William's inspiration was probably less a divine vision than the fear of the growing power of the archbishop of Palermo.

The archbishop was a resourceful Englishman named Walter of the Mill, who had united nearly every important baron and prelate of the kingdom behind him to form a power second only to that of the king. Moreover, as archbishop, he was the link between William and the pope, and William was understandably uneasy at Walter's independence and influence. The king thus attempted to curb this threat to his own power by creating a new archbishopric, as close as possible to Palermo. Normally any such appointment would have required Walter's approval. William, however, managed to bypass Walter. He founded a Benedictine monastery and elected an abbot of his own choosing.

To increase the prestige of the newly appointed abbot, William showered him with titles and privileges, including a baronetcy, several feudal castles and villages, and five fishing boats in the harbor of Palermo. Because of the political urgency of William's situation, the cathedral at Monreale, formally known as the Cathedral of Santa Maria La Nuova, was completed in fifteen years, from 1174 to 1189. Its basic style is Romanesque, but the harmonious incorporation of Byzantine and Islamic elements makes it a fascinating architectural hybrid.

Two square Norman towers flank the façade. The nave is that of a typical Italian basilica, with a timber roof and two side aisles divided from the nave by rows of slender columns, all culminating at the east end in a massive, triple-apsed Romanesque sanctuary.

Imposed upon this basically Western church are "foreign" elements, such as the Islamic exterior of the three semicircular eastern apses. They are ornamented with tiers of small columns and interlacing, mosaicked arches of alternating black and white stone. The delicate form of these arches foreshadows the development of the Gothic style in Europe.

Inside the cathedral, the continuation of Byzantine influence within Norman Sicily is overwhelmingly demonstrated by the mosaics which cover almost every available surface. They are estimated to cover an area of 70,400 square feet and constitute one of the largest surviving examples of this Byzantine form. The mosaics in the nave and side aisles depict scenes from the Old Testament, prophesying the coming of Christ. They relate episodes from the lives of the Apostles on the arches of the transept, and others from the life of Christ in each transept. Many of the figures are huge, especially that of Christ Pantocrator in the half dome of the apse. Christ's upheld hand, which measures six feet in height, seems to reach out and bless the vast expanse of the church. The figure of the enthroned Virgin below it is flanked by two angels and the Apostles. Beneath this tableau are the figures of fourteen saints. Among them are a few surprises, including the earliest known representation of Thomas à Becket dating from less than a generation after his death in 1170. It is commonly thought that Becket was included at Monreale because of the desire of William's queen to atone for the conduct of her father, Henry II of England, who was responsible for Becket's death.

Becket's is only one of several politically motivated mosaics, most of which pay deliberate tribute to other episcopal saints and martyrs. One famous mosaic cycle above the royal throne shows King William receiving the crown directly from Christ rather than from the pope. All the mosaics at Monreale are on a dazzling gold background. The effects of the gold, woven throughout the brilliantly colored mosaic scenes, seem to symbolize the golden age that Norman rule brought to Sicily.

Unlike the mosaics, the bronze doors of the cathedral do not show a marked Byzantine influence. In fact, they are the beginning of a more sculptural, indigenous Italian style. Sculpted in 1186 by artists from Tuscany, including Bonanno Pisano, the doors are divided into forty-two bas-relief panels depicting scenes of early Christian and secular history.

Except for its great central cloister, the Benedictine monastery built by William

Below left, a plan of the entire abbey complex at Monreale. The cathedral is to the left of the large square cloister. Above the cloister is the archbishop's palace, to its right are the remains of the medieval refectory, and below it is the seminary which is found there today. This Benedictine monastery first opened its doors in the spring of 1136 when William II brought in one hundred monks from La Cava to colonize Monreale.

Below, the little arcade that encloses the fountain in the northwest corner of the cloister. This is one of the most tranquil and poetic spots at Monreale.

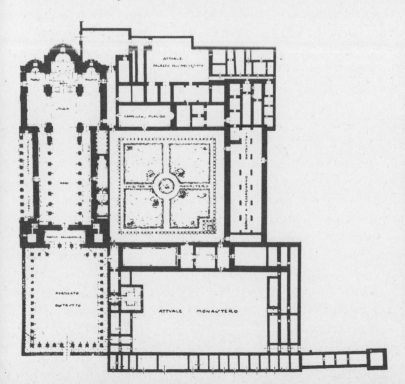

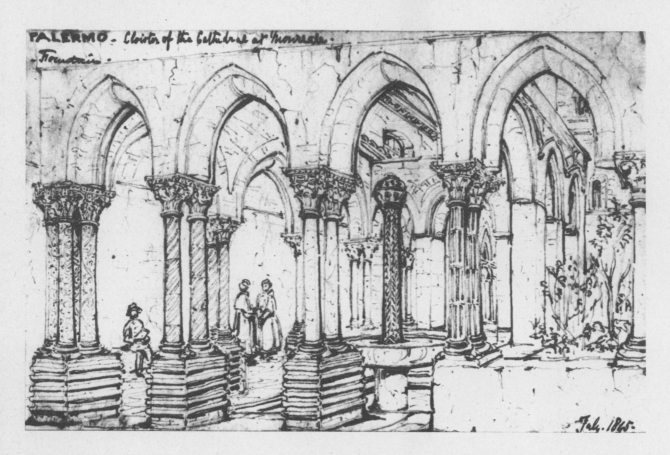

PALERMO. Cloister of the Cathedral at Monreale. Fountain.

Feb. 1845.

Above, a sketch of the cloister and fountain at Monreale, drawn in 1845 by a British traveler.

beside the cathedral is mostly in ruins. This perfectly square garden, measuring 170 feet on each side, is a masterpiece. The garden's 228 paired columns supporting the roof of the covered walkway are an example of Romanesque stone carving unequaled in Sicily. Most of the capitals belong to the Norman period, though some were carved as late as the sixteenth century. Many of the scenes portrayed are secular, even pagan, but most typical of the time are the Biblical stories and moral tales designed for religious contemplation. One well-known inscription on a capital, illustrating the life of Lazarus, warns: *O dives, dives, non multo tempore vives* ("O rich man, rich man, you shall not live for long").

There is also an Arabic influence in the 104 slim arches over the columns which are carved or inlaid with marble and mosaic. The fountain in the southwest corner of the cloister, of finely crafted marble, displays the same influence—particularly in the cluster of small lion-head spouts which surmount it.

Preserved within the cathedral are many sacred relics, including pieces of a belt purportedly worn by Saint Thomas Aquinas and the remains of Saint Castrensis, who was said to have sailed the seas in a boat with no bottom. Here are the tombs of William I (William the Bad) and that of his more exemplary son. William II's body was laid to rest at Monreale after a long and acrimonious struggle with his long-time enemy Walter of the Mill, who insisted that the king's sarcophagus be placed in his own new cathedral at Palermo. Though the king's remains were finally removed to Monreale, Walter successfully retained the sarcophagus in Palermo.

The Norman dynasty in Sicily came to an end with William II's death in 1189, the same year in which the cathedral at Monreale was completed. William died childless. He had named as his heir his aunt Constance, wife of the Holy Roman Emperor Henry VI. However, the Sicilian nobles, wishing to prevent German rule in Sicily, chose Constance's nephew, Tancred of Lecce, as William's successor. Tancred ruled the kingdom until his death, when Henry was crowned king. Sicily thus became part of the Holy Roman Empire, but after Henry's death, all of Italy revolted against German rule. Constance renounced German kingship for her infant son Frederick and had him crowned king of Sicily in 1198.

William left behind a progressive kingdom, one said to have been the richest and best organized state in Italy. The stability and tolerance that characterized Norman rule insured the survival and eventual fusion of diverse traditions, which combined to form a strong and creative kingdom. The cathedral at Monreale, which epitomizes the eclectic architecture of the Norman period, marks a turning point in the aesthetic and intellectual fortunes of Europe. In its delicate proportions and in the way it introduces pointed Arabic arches in a still predominantly Romanesque style, it presages the hopeful verticality of cathedral architecture which was soon to develop in France. Above all, Monreale stands as one of the best expressions of a brief and brilliant period of Mediterranean civilization which prospered under the unlikely rule of the blond conquerors from the north.

Santiago de Compostela

Spain

Throughout the Middle Ages, Santiago de Compostela in northwest Spain was the goal of countless thousands of pilgrims, most of whom made the 900-mile journey from France on foot. They came to pay homage to Saint James the Great, whose bones were believed to have been buried there. Even now, particularly during Jubilee Years when the Apostle's feast day falls on a Sunday, the vast Plaza del Obradoiro facing the Cathedral of Santiago de Compostela (preceding page) is thronged with pilgrims commemorating Saint James.

The Cathedral of Santiago de Compostela is the largest and most complete Romanesque church in Spain. Built between 1070 and 1124, it reflects the considerable influence of French architecture of the time. The cathedral's ornate façade (right), an eighteenth-century addition, was erected by Fernando Casas y Novoa and is one of the finest examples of the extreme Spanish Baroque style known as Churrigueresque.

Above left, an equestrian figure representing Santiago Matamoros, or Saint James the Moor-Slayer, and the coat of arms of a cardinal-archbishop of Compostela that adorns the Grand Stairway leading to the cathedral's main entrance. Above, a knocker on one of the brass-studded doors of the cathedral's western façade. Below left, the western side of the mid-sixteenth-century cloister adjacent to the cathedral.

Immediately inside the cathedral is the late twelfth-century Portico de la Gloria (near right), the work of the master Mateo. Many scholars cite these sculptures as the first to have been executed in the Gothic style. Crouching beasts supporting the columns of the doorjamb (below) are more typical of the cathedral's predominant Romanesque style. The figure of Saint James (above) stands on the tripartite portico, which depicts the Last Judgment. A large figure of Christ (above far right) dominates the central tympanum of the portico. The emergence of the Gothic sensibility is most evident in the realistic expressions of the Apostles Peter, Paul, James, and John (below far right).

The simplicity of the cathedral's Romanesque nave (left) stands in marked contrast to the later Baroque façade. In the Middle Ages the cathedral was rarely this tranquil since it was customary for pilgrims to camp for days in the side aisles and triforium balconies.

The sixteenth-century cloister (below left and below), located off the south transept of the cathedral, ranks among the most severely beautiful in Spain. The walkways are 115 feet long and 19 feet wide.

Saint James's relics rest in a crypt within the Capilla Mayor (right), the sanctuary of the cathedral. Today the revered statue of the saint, which stands directly over the crypt, is dwarfed by the magnificence of the Churrigueresque high altar. Indeed, the extravagant retable and the eighteenth-century twin pipe organs completely transform the Romanesque interior.

The entrance to the south transept of the cathedral, the Puerta de Platerías (left), is the church's only remaining Romanesque façade. Although a victim of haphazard restoration, many of its original sculptures survive, including the carved tympanum (below left), statuary figures of Christ (above), and King David (below).

Above right, a statue of Saint James over the early seventeenth-century Puerta Santa. The saint is dressed as a pilgrim to his own shrine and flanked by smaller figures of his disciples Saint Athanasius and Saint Theodosius. This holy door is opened only during Jubilee Years. The twenty-four prophets and Apostles arranged on either side of the Puerta Santa (detail, right) date from the construction of the cathedral and may be the work of Mateo. Above, the Puerta Real, built in 1657 by master Peña de Toro.

Intricately carved twelfth-century capitals from the cathedral's Puerto de Platerías (following page) testify to the artistic influence of the powerful French Cluniac monastic movement, which filtered into this remote corner of Spain.

Santiago de Compostela Spain

Give me my scallop shell of quiet,
My staff of faith to walk upon,
My scrip of joy, immortal diet,
My bottle of salvation,
My gown of glory, hope's true gage;
And thus I'll make my pilgrimage...

These lines by Sir Walter Raleigh introduce an allegorical poem that describes the soul's pilgrimage over "silver mountains" to a "spring of immortality." They are also a remarkably accurate description of the pilgrim garb—a heavy cape, an eight-foot-long staff with an empty gourd to carry water, and a broad-brimmed hat decorated with scallop shells—worn by countless thousands of Christians who have made the sacred journey over the

Way of St. James, the road to Santiago de Compostela.

Santiago de Compostela was so important in the medieval world that originally the word pilgrim applied only to those who took up the Way of St. James. The holy shrine of Saint James in northwestern Spain was long one of the most visited pilgrimage sites in Christendom. Legend says that this once-remote region was brought out of obscurity in 814, the year a hermit named Pelayo saw a supernaturally brilliant star shining above an unplowed Galician field. When the star reappeared over the same spot on several successive nights, the hermit informed his superior, Bishop Theodomir, who ordered an excavation of the site. A small tomb containing human remains was discovered, which caused an immediate sensation: surely these were the long-sought remains of the Apostle and patron of Spain, Saint James the Great.

According to widely accepted tradition, the original disciples of Jesus dispersed after the Ascension to preach the gospel in distant lands. Saint James the Great, the brother of Saint John, was supposed to have made his way to Iberia where he made many converts. He is then said to have returned to Jerusalem and his sub-

sequent martyrdom. The Spanish people, however, were never reconciled to the loss of their patron and, in time, another tradition grew up. This claimed that, after James's death, two of his disciples carried the saint's body back to Galicia in northwestern Spain where a tomb was provided to house the saint's bones and, eventually, those of the disciples as well. On the basis of these stories, Bishop Theodomir was quick to proclaim his find as the lost grave of Saint James, and his countrymen were happy to believe him.

The time was propitious for the return of Spain's patron saint, since it provided Iberian Christians with a unifying symbol of their resistance against Moslem invaders. Quite soon, the gentle Saint James was metamorphosed into Santiago Matamoros, or Saint James the Moor-Slayer. The story was told that Santiago, riding a white steed and brandishing a sword, had appeared at the Battle of Clavijo in 934 to urge King Ramiro on to victory against a force of 70,000 infidels. Historians are not sure whether this battle actually took place, but from this time on, Santiago's

Below, the town of Santiago de Compostela dominated by its massive cathedral.

name became the battle cry of Spanish soldiers in the centuries-long struggle against the Moors and, later, in New Spain.

In the meantime, the site of Santiago's tomb was becoming increasingly important as a place of worship. Around the shrine there grew up a small town, Compostela, whose name is said—poetically—to be a corruption of the Latin, *campus stellae*, or "starry field." Etymologists endorse the less romantic explanation that it derives from *compostela*, meaning "burial ground."

Though the Moors managed to capture Santiago de Compostela in 997, the town was back in Christian hands by the eleventh century and was receiving the estimated half a million pilgrims a year who made their way along the road to the shrine of Saint James. The road itself was popularly known as *la voie lactée*, or "the milky way"—some say because of the countless souls that traveled it, others because in the early summer the real Milky Way hung over the road like a canopy,

pointing to the saint's shrine in the west.

From about 1017 onward, pilgrimage to Santiago de Compostela received powerful support from two sources: the papacy and the Benedictine monastery of Cluny in central France. Rome encouraged the cult of Santiago because of the importance of winning Spain back from the Moors. In fact, Spanish knights were excused from the Crusades in the Holy Land so they could join in the struggle. Then in 1122, Pope Calixtus II declared that Santiago could celebrate a Jubilee Year each year in which St. James's feast day, July 25, falls on a Sunday. This privilege, still enjoyed today, gave the site a major advantage over Rome, where only every twenty-fifth year is a Jubilee.

But it was the support of the Cluniac monks which did the most to assure Santiago de Compostela's importance. Perhaps motivated by the desire to extend their influence into northern Spain, the brothers of Cluny made it their business to organize pilgrimages, providing conven-

Left, miniatures of Spanish monarchs who fought the Moors. From left to right, Alfonso V of Leon who died fighting in Portugal in 1027; Ferdinand I of Castile who defeated the emirs of Toledo and Seville; and Alfonso VI of Leon and Castile who reconquered Toledo. During his reign, Santiago's cathedral was begun.

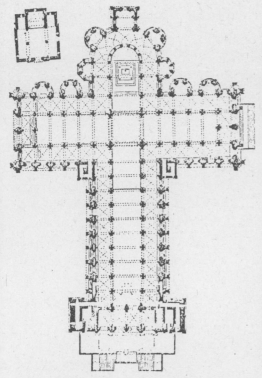

iently placed inns and hostels down the length of France and across northern Spain. Eventually, they even wrote a guidebook, called the *Codex Calixtus,* which collected various legends about Santiago and described the route.

By this time, the official beginning of the Way of St. James was in Paris where pilgrims of all stations gathered to begin the 900-mile journey. Farther south, the road branched into four separate routes. The pilgrims traveled on foot, averaging up to thirty miles daily. The four roads converged at the Pass of Roncesvalles in the Pyrenees. Here, in northern Spain, travel became difficult indeed, both because of the poverty of the country and the multitude of bandits. Even the English, who often avoided some of the walking by traveling the first leg of the journey by sea, found the route formidable. As a fifteenth-century English pilgrim named Purchase wrote: "Men may leve all gamys, when saylen to Seynt Jamys."

The association between Cluny and Santiago de Compostela proved profitable for both. Around 1070 construction began on the Cathedral of Santiago. By the early part of the twelfth century, the town's first archbishop, the energetic Diego Gelmirez, had both completed the cathedral and built the broad Plaza Obradoiro in front.

Above left, the cathedral's floor plan with its radiating chapels and broad transepts typical of pilgrimage churches. Above right, the sixteenth-century cloisters.

Left, a twelfth-century Romanesque bas-relief of Saint James from the Puerta de Platerías. the entrance to the south transept. Right, part of the exterior of the apse.

All of this was financed in an interesting way. In the twelfth century, Santiago ecclesiastics conveniently discovered a document signed by the ninth-century King Ramirez ordering all provinces liberated from the Moors to make an annual offering in perpetuity to Santiago Matamoros. This tax, collected regularly until 1834, gave the cathedral an independent source of income to carry out continual renovations and additions.

The first fruits of Santiago's inheritance went into raising a Romanesque cathedral unlike any in Spain. Its original master builder, Bernard the Marvelous, was al-

most certainly French and a student of Cluny architecture, as was his famous follower, the master Mateo.

It was Mateo who created the cathedral's great masterpiece, the Portico de la Gloria. In effect a vestibule, the portico consists of three sets of elaborately sculpted doorways that stand just inside the main entrance of the cathedral and lead to the nave. The pillar in the center of the portico's main door is carved to represent the Tree of Jesse. It has been worn smooth by the hands of thousands of pilgrims who traditionally touch the pillar as a sign of their journey's end. On the interior side of the pillar, half-hidden in the dim light of the nave, squats a carved figure of Mateo himself. This too is revered by pilgrims who touch the statue's head for luck upon leaving the church. The lifelike features of Mateo's sculptures are the first triumph of the Gothic. Indeed, the Cluniac masters may have brought the Romanesque style to Spain, but they returned to France bearing the message of Gothic realism.

As is common for a pilgrimage church, the Cathedral of Santiago de Compostela is studded with small niches and chapels that hold a variety of relics—including a "thorn from the Crown of Thorns" and even a phial of "the Virgin's milk." Some of these devotional objects are modern, such as the statue of the Virgin crowned with a halo of electric lights. Equally medieval in inspiration—although modern in fact—is *el botafumiero,* a giant silver incense burner that is swung in great arcs over the heads of the worshipers. The work of a nineteenth-century silversmith,

Below, an engraving of a procession of pilgrims on the route to Santiago de Compostela. Below right, an eleventh-century fresco of a pilgrim.

it follows a design established in medieval times when incense was thought to protect worshipers against the plague.

The Capilla Mayor—the sanctuary of the church that holds the painted and bejeweled statue of Saint James—is the central focus of the cathedral, though it is the crypt, beneath the magnificent Baroque high altar, that is of primary interest to the faithful.

The crypt holds the bones believed to be those of the Apostle. As long as the Moors threatened Spain, few dared to impugn the character of Santiago Matamoros. But after 1492, skeptics slowly began to come forward. The learned Erasmus wrote a dialogue questioning the basis of the Saint James legends, and ordinary Christians expressed their growing doubts by staying home. The tide of pilgrims began to ebb in the sixteenth century, when the bones were lost after having been hidden away during an attack on La Coruña by Sir Francis Drake in 1584. By the time of the Carlist Wars of the nineteenth century, the shrine had essentially been abandoned. Then in 1879, Cardinal Payá y Rico decided to clear Santiago's reputation once and for all. He ordered an excavation of the sealed tomb, just above the site of the original crypt, where the bones of the saint

and his two disciples were said to have been hidden. To the delight of the faithful, the tomb was found to contain the remains of three men.

The problem arose, however, of having to prove that these ancient bones actually belonged to Saint James and his followers, Athanasius and Theodosius. By matching one of the skulls with a fragment that had been preserved elsewhere as a relic, a special commission from Rome concluded that the bones were indeed authentic. In 1884, Pope Leo XIII gave the renewed pilgrimage to Santiago de Compostela his approval, and a stream of modern pilgrims began to arrive, some electing to travel the last part of the route on foot.

No matter how one arrives, to be in Santiago de Compostela on July 25, and especially on July 25 of a Jubilee Year, is well worth the trip. The pageantry includes processions of masked figures, a ceremonial lighting of *el botafumiero,* and richly gowned prelates celebrating a special twelfth-century mass of Saint James taken from the *Codex Calixtus.* Eleven centuries after the hermit Pelayo saw his miraculous star, the Way of St. James toward Santiago is still the earthly counterpart of the Milky Way—paved with souls instead of stars.

Rila

Bulgaria

The red-roofed monastery at Rila (preceding page) nestles in the thick woods of Bulgaria's Rila Planina mountain range. Its irregular layout is a necessary adaptation to the mountainous terrain. The monastery's sheer perpendicular walls and towers, with their high windows (top far left), were designed to ward off bands of roaming brigands. Though the exterior has a solid, fortresslike appearance, the façades facing into the monastery courtyard (center far left) consist of inviting open arcades.

Within the courtyard stands the monastery church (remaining photos) dating from the 1830s. Its basic form is that of a four-domed cross with two side chapels. The total arrangement, however, is extremely complex, with no fewer than twenty-four domes. The church is given even greater richness by the striping of the exterior and the alternating black and white stripes of the porch.

Bottom far left, the Samokov Gate in the eastern wall, one of the two entrances to the monastery.

After passing through the Samokov Gate into the interior of the monastery, you reach the northern residential block (above left). This is the longest wing of the complex, and perhaps the most elaborate architecturally, with double arcades on the eastern end and a triple layer of arches on the western—all crowned by a wooden balcony.

The western façade of the church (below left) reveals diverse cultural influences. The masonry striping is distinctively Turkish; the domes and curving roof derive from Byzantine models; and the arches and columns are Western in origin.

The Hreljo Tower (right), the oldest structure in the monastery, was built in 1353 as a fortification for the monks by Hreljo Dragovol, the local feudal lord. Its stern aspect, with tall, narrow windows, battlemented top, and bold system of buttresses, is somewhat relieved by the playful brickwork in and around the buttress arches. The decorated porch on the western end dates from the nineteenth century.

The monastery church houses perhaps the best examples anywhere of nineteenth-century Bulgarian religious painting. The interior of the porch (above) is completely covered with frescoes. Top left, the Archangel Michael taking the rich man's soul. Center left, the martyr Saint Nicholas from Myra, Asia Minor. Above near right, the Virgin and Child, surrounded by a host of saints. Above far right, Saint Ivan of Rila, founder of the monastery. Bottom far right, the parable of Lazarus and the poor man.

The monastery of Rila is a rich repository of Bulgarian culture. It has an extensive library and a valuable collection of artworks. Left, the gilt-silver cover of the Krupnik Gospel, made in 1640 by the master Matei of Sofia. The gospel was given to the monastery in 1577 by the bishop of Krupnik. Center far right, the first page of the Gospel according to Saint Luke in the Krupnik Gospel.

Near right, a parchment miniature of Saint Matthew the Evangelist, from the Sutschavo Gospel (1529). He is portrayed as a contemporary Bulgarian scribe. Top far right, a seventeenth-century manuscript illustration executed on damask of Saint John the Baptist baptizing Christ.

The monastery also contains celebrated Bulgarian woodcarvings. The flowing, naturalistic plant motifs (below left) on the ceiling of the Koprivshtitsa Room are often cited as the finest example of nineteenth-century craftsmanship in Bulgaria. Below, the gilded, wooden central panel of the iconostasis, the screen which separates the sanctuary from the main body of the church. Its exuberance, like that of the carved pulpit (below near right), is typical of the nascent Bulgarian nationalism that emerged during the early nineteenth century.

Below far right, detail of one of the small bas-relief panels of the altar cross in the church. Carved by the monk Raphael from 1790 to 1802, the ten panels of the cross and surrounding scrollwork depict over a thousand figures in Biblical scenes.

Rila Bulgaria

The monastery at Rila stands on a remote mountain side in western Bulgaria. Lost among the clear lakes and peaks of the Rila Planina mountain range, the isolated cluster of buildings is one of the finest surviving monuments to Bulgarian architecture and painting. The country's newly awakened interest in Rila, and the heritage it represents, reflects a trend among all Balkan countries: the rediscovery of native cultural traditions. Dating from the past century or so, this consciousness was both reflected and accelerated by a newfound enthusiasm for peasant culture, folklore, and history.

Because of its isolation in the moun-
tains, Rila monastery was a popular refuge during Bulgaria's frequent occupations by foreign tribes and conquerors. The country, originally ancient Thrace and Moesia, was settled by the Slavs in the sixth century A.D. Toward the end of the seventh century, Bulgar tribes from the banks of the Volga crossed the lower Danube in the southern Balkans. In time, they subjugated the Slavs, adopted their language and culture, and settled permanently in the country.

Christianity soon spread among the Bulgars, both from their Greek and Slavonic subjects and from the states on the west and north. By the middle of the ninth century, after considerable discord, the Bulgarian ruler Boris I adopted Christianity. For a short time, the Bulgarians belonged to the Byzantine church, but by A.D. 870, the independence of the Bulgarian church had come to be recognized by Constantinople.

Christianity was the official religion, but it was not free from corruption. Ivan of Rila, who was born six years after Bulgaria adopted Christianity, was an early critic of the church. Of aristocratic parentage and highly educated, Ivan was so dissatisfied
by the worldliness and impiety of the Bulgarian court and clergy that he retired alone to the isolation of the Rila mountains at the age of twenty.

Ivan's reputation gradually spread. As was often the case with such holy men, he attracted increasing numbers of disciples and pilgrims. When a monastic community began to develop near his dwelling, Ivan again retreated, this time to a tiny cave, where he died in 946.

The first small community settled by Ivan's followers stood several miles from the present site in a region isolated from political and economic currents. Roads and settlements were scarce, as were food and fodder. Since Rila was originally more a collection of hermitages than a centralized monastery, it attracted those who rejected the active life for one of contemplation, individual prayer, and lengthy liturgical services.

Below, an engraving of the monastery, dated 1836. One of the most vital centers of the Orthodox religion, even in the darkest times of Turkish domination, the monastery became a symbol of the Bulgarian renaissance in the nineteenth century.

Above, a portrait of Saint Ivan of Rila made in 1946 on the thousandth anniversary of his death. Right, an engraving of 1847, showing the monastery and significant episodes in the saint's life. This design was later used for postage stamps. An engraving of 1839 (below right) shows the Madonna between Saint Nicholas (left) and Saint Ivan.

Some monks lived in the main building. Others built their own dwellings, generally small huts that barely withstood the harsh winters. They lived on such food as they could grow and beg or buy from visiting pilgrims and merchants. Many monasteries conducted regular fairs, which attracted flocks of visitors; Rila did not. Its income seems to have been augmented by substantial gifts and occasional bequests from laymen.

During the eleventh and twelfth centuries, the gradual but steady decline of the Bulgarian empire paralleled a decline at Rila. Fewer alms were received from pilgrims, as travel was inhibited by banditry, political turmoil, and foreign invaders. It was only during the thirteenth and early fourteenth centuries, when the Bulgars overthrew Byzantine domination and established a new empire, that the monastery began to prosper again.

In 1335, the local feudal prince, Hreljo, chose to live in the monastery grounds. He

constructed various buildings, including a small church in the courtyard and a five-story stone tower. None has survived except the tower, which was intended as a personal refuge. Ironically enough, he was assassinated there in 1343.

The fourteenth century saw a shift in the character of the Rila monastery, with a growing emphasis on culture, scholarship, and economic possessions. Its property, which included vineyards, meadows, pastures, mills, and other sources of revenue, was exempted from taxation. The spirituality of earlier years now was matched by temporal concerns. This mood continued

Above, the seal of the monastery, which depicts Saint Ivan.

Right, a late nineteenth-century Romantic painting of the monastery.

after 1396, when the Ottoman Turks swept into the Balkans and completely occupied Bulgaria.

Turkish rule was often oppressive and rebellions were frequent. The Turks undermined the very basis of independent Bulgarian culture by recognizing the authority of the Eastern Orthodox Church in Constantinople over all the Christians in their empire. But for the most part, the Ottoman rulers did not insist on converting their subjects to Islam. They were much more interested in collecting regular tax revenues and maintaining a docile and productive citizenry.

Some of the monks of Rila fled the first Turkish invaders. Others stayed to hide the monastery's heritage of precious jewels, books, and documents. They were reassured when the sultans reinstated the privileges previously granted by the Bulgarian czars. But during the second quarter of the fifteenth century, the monastery was subject to Moslem religious violence and frequent attacks by bandits. Buildings were looted and destroyed and monks killed or forced to flee. For several years, the monastery was abandoned—the only break in its entire history. Though the persecutions ended within a generation and the monks returned to rebuild what had been destroyed, the sultans in Con-

stantinople never succeeded in insuring their security.

Literary activity increased in the sixteenth century, as the monks copied old manuscripts and wrote chronicles. The contemporary written language, known as Bulgarian Church Slavonic, had been created by Saint Cyril and Saint Methodius in the ninth century for their translation of the gospels. The use of Church Slavonic also strengthened an affiliation with Russia, the only substantial Orthodox political and military power. At this same time, delegations from Rila traveled directly to Moscow to seek subsidies.

Rila desperately needed money. As the Ottoman Empire declined in the seventeenth century, local Turkish officials demanded increasingly heavy taxes. Internal order disappeared; Moslem bandits looted and extorted; and Christian outlaws roamed the mountains, seeking revenge—and cash—from affluent Moslems. Monasteries often provided food and shelter for Christians on the run. Secret meetings were held in them, when emissaries from Austria and Russia—who were periodically at war with the Turks—came in search of support from the Balkan Christians.

Some old photographs of the interior of the monastery. The ground floors were occupied by storerooms, kitchens (a ceiling below) and dining rooms, bakeries, and study rooms; the upper floors contained sleeping quarters. Near right, the interior of the ground-floor arcade of the eastern wing. Far right, the corridor on the second floor of the western wing.

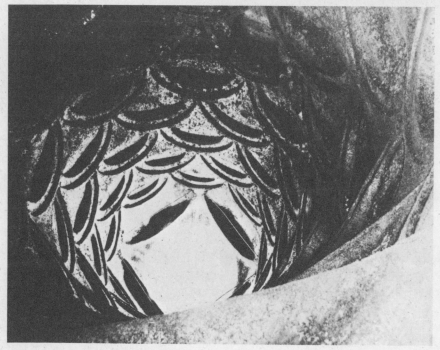

The role played by the Rila monastery in clandestine politics paved the way for its part in the Bulgarian cultural and political awakening of the late eighteenth and nineteenth centuries. Rila became the very symbol of Bulgarian nationalism as well as a literary center for the modern Bulgarian language.

As a result, more space was needed to accommodate pilgrims, in addition to new monks and students training for the priesthood. Expansion began about 1749 and continued by stages until 1784. Several churches were also built in the surrounding mountains, often to commemorate events in the life of Ivan of Rila.

From 1816 to 1870, much additional construction was undertaken by laborers organized into independent bands under a leader. Like mercenaries, they traveled around the country in search of construction work. At Rila, these roving workers built three of the four encircling dormitory blocks of the monastery between 1816 and 1819. The shorter south wing was added late in the 1840s, enclosing the courtyard.

Local building materials were used throughout: pine, beech, and oak timbers, boulders and river stones for foundations and outside walls, limestone for mortar, and clay for bricks and tiles. The de facto architect in the early years was one master Alexi, who in a symbolic break with tradition, announced his achievements in three wall slabs. He was a new type of Bulgar-

ian—the age of subservience was ending, that of individualism was beginning.

A fire early in 1833 destroyed the wooden sections of the new wings, but the brick and stone walls survived, and the monastery quickly recovered. Money and labor for reconstruction flooded in from throughout the country, in what became a great manifestation of nationalism. Groups of bricklayers, stonemasons, carpenters, and others traveled for days with their families to settle temporarily at the monastery and contribute their skills. Work continued into the winter and was completed early in 1834. The church built by Hreljo in the fourteenth century, which was too small for current needs, was dismantled and replaced by a much larger, lavishly decorated building. In the process, its unique frescoes were destroyed. Frescoes, murals, and carvings in stone and wood play an important decorative role in many of the new buildings. The themes were, inevitably, religious and didactic, though rendered with an original vigor and native skill that reflected a larger phenomenon: the confidence of a new generation of Bulgarians.

Bulgaria finally achieved independence in 1878. During the dark years of Ottoman oppression, the monasteries, and Rila in particular, had become the repositories of national feeling, hope, and pride. Without them, present-day Bulgaria might not have come into being, and the Bulgarians might not have survived as a nation.